JUNG'S PSYCHOLOGY
AS A SPIRITUAL PRACTICE
AND WAY OF LIFE

A Dialogue

William D. Geoghegan

with
Kevin L. Stoehr

Edited by Kevin L. Stoehr

Kevin L Stoehr

For Paula —
with much love
& best wishes,
Kevin
12-03

University Press of America,® Inc.
Lanham · New York · Oxford

University Press of America,® Inc.
4720 Boston Way
Lanham, Maryland 20706

PO Box 317
Oxford
OX2 9RU, UK

Library of Congress Cataloging-in-Publication Data

Geoghegan, William D., 1922-
Jung's psychology as a spiritual practice and a way of life :
a dialogue / William D. Geoghegan with Kevin L. Stoehr ;
edited by Kevin L. Stoehr.
p. cm.
Includes bibliographical references.
1. Psychoanalysis and religion. 2. Jung, C. G. (Carl Gustav),
1875-1961. 3. Geoghegan, William, D., 1922- --Interviews.
4. Religion historians—United States—Interviews.
5. Self-realization—Religious aspects. 6. Nihilism—Religious
aspects. 7. Laozi. Dao de jing. I. Stoehr, Kevin L., 1967- II. Title.

BF175.4.R44 G46 2002
150.19'54—dc21   2002032327 CIP

ISBN 0-7618-2418-9 (paperback : alk. ppr.)

DEDICATION

This book is dedicated to my beloved wife, Betty,

Sarah Elizabeth Phelps Geoghegan

WDG

TABLE OF CONTENTS

PREFACE

This book considers the pioneering depth-psychologist Carl Gustav Jung, primarily as a sage of world-class stature. It focuses on Jung as an archetypal wisdom teacher, in three important respects:

(1) in the post-modern West, primarily in interaction with Friedrich Nietzsche and his *Thus Spake Zarathustra* and also with theologian Paul Tillich and Zen master Karlfried Graf Dürckheim;

(2) in his deep spiritual kinship with the timeless universality of Lao-tze and his classic *The Tao Te Ching*;

(3) and in consideration of the future prospects of Jung's psychology in mind/body medicine, especially neuroscience, and in dialogue with quantum speculation.

This book contends that Jung's psychology is not primarily a form of psychotherapy in the conventional sense but essentially a dynamic "religious philosophical system" constituting a spiritual practice and way of life.

The dialogue format suggests not only Jung's own dialogue or "confrontation" with the Unconscious but also his generally unacknowledged spiritual affinity with the central Western philosophical tradition, a tradition stemming from Socrates and Plato and their devotion to the task of "living the questions."

William D. Geoghegan
Brunswick, Maine
2002

ACKNOWLEDGEMENTS

While many persons have co-operated to make this book possible, I wish especially to acknowledge the following:

Richard Guy Miller, artist and world-traveler, who for more than a decade audited and taped my courses and irrepressibly pestered me into writing the book;

Kevin L. Stoehr, indispensable dialogue partner and editor;

Michael Mastronardi, attorney, publisher, and entrepreneur who voluntarily assumed the task of overseeing the production and distribution of this work, and his lovely wife **Bonnie**, who executed the layout and details of the very impressive cover design;

Thomas B. Cornell, Richard F. Steele Professor of Studio Art at Bowdoin College and vigorous partner in our quarter-century Plato-Nietzsche dialogue, who volunteered to do the cover art concept;

Gerlinde W. Rickel, academic co-ordinator, whose expert professional services for many years have been invaluable in assisting me in all aspects of my academic work;

Walter R. Christie, Dean F. Davies, Paul D. Huss, Rabbi Harry Sky, and **Murray Stein**, who all graciously agreed to read significant portions of the manuscript and to offer their kind comments.

Finally, special thanks to all of my friends in the **Bowdoin College Jung Seminar**, the **Brunswick Jung Center, First Parish Church** and the Brunswick community in general.

William D. Geoghegan
Brunswick, Maine
2002

Special Note: Any royalties that are paid to the authors from the sale of this book will be donated exclusively to the William D. Geoghegan Scholarship Fund at Bowdoin College.

INTRODUCTION: ULTIMATE CONCERN

by
Kevin L. Stoehr

The book that you are now holding in your hands is very much in the tradition of Platonic dialogue writing, and the philosophical vision that it attempts to express is, at its roots, very much a Socratic one. But it is also a unique dialogue with a unique and inspirational teaching about spirituality at its core. There are two interlocutors in the conversation that is about to unfold. There is a distinguished professor of religion who has recently retired after over forty years of liberal arts teaching and there is a young professor of philosophy who was once the undergraduate student of his elder dialogue partner. Mirrored by the dialogue form itself, this is a conversation about crossing boundaries, lived wisdom, and the mutual arising of spiritual insights.

Both characters are drawn from real-life figures, who are in fact the authors of this very dialogue. Bill Geoghegan is an emeritus Professor of Religion at Bowdoin College in Maine, the founder of the Bowdoin College Jung Seminar (1980), and a co-founder of the Bowdoin-Brunswick C. G. Jung Center for Studies in Analytical Psychology (1990). I currently teach a year-long course in ethics, existentialism, and depth-psychology at Boston University.

The dialogue itself is an intricate tapestry that has been creatively woven together from transcriptions of oral lectures by Professor Geoghegan, from my own research and ruminations, and from an on-going series of dialogues and correspondence between us. What we have attempted to do here is to present a unified conversation that begins with fundamental questions about human nature and that leads through various twists and turns – questions, answers, arguments, and speculations – to the articulation of an overall philosophical teaching about spirituality. This teaching, which takes as its departure point the broad perspective of Jungian psychology, concerns the nature of human spiritedness and self-realization in the face of those moral and spiritual challenges that have irrupted into contemporary society.

This is a conversation about *ultimate concern*, to use theologian Paul Tillich's term for the most serious of our spiritual and philosophical engagements.[1] It is a book about our confrontations with the specter of Nothingness or Non-Being and with the brute contingencies in our everyday lives. It is a dialogue about finding our way through the moral and existential "wilderness" of our contemporary humanity. It is a conversation about the pressing problem of nihilism and about possible ways of overcoming that problem.

I have participated in a heart-felt dialogue over a number of years with my former professor. Bill Geoghegan inspired me when I was an undergraduate major in philosophy. His life-long love of the liberal arts has continued to inspire me over the years since my days at Bowdoin College. One of the major reasons why I decided to become a teacher of philosophy and religion was because of my enthusiasm for Bill's charismatic way of teaching these subjects.

I first met Bill in the autumn of 1986. I was undertaking a free-lance assignment for *The Orient*, Bowdoin's weekly student-run newspaper, during my first semester at the College. It proved to be my initial encounter with a remarkable teacher of philosophy and religion and, underlying the traditional academic subject matter, with a man who communicated clearly the value of both spiritedness and spirituality.

I had been asked to cover an upcoming meeting of the Bowdoin Jung Seminar. The Seminar met regularly on Tuesday afternoons in the Faculty Room of Massachusetts Hall. My first article for *The Orient* had been a story on restoration efforts in reclaiming the nearby Androscoggin River from environmental damage. I knew a bit about the Androscoggin, since I was born and raised in southern Maine and knew the river well. My next task proved to be much more daunting.

I knew absolutely nothing about Bill Geoghegan, the founder and leader of the Seminar, and almost nothing about the famed Swiss psychologist Carl Gustav Jung (1875-1961). As I was to learn, Jung had once been the chosen "heir apparent" of Sigmund Freud but had broken dramatically from his mentor by renouncing Freud's over-emphasis on the libido. Jung had gone on to establish his own brand of psychotherapy, which he called "analytical psychology," based upon a theory that put the role of sexuality in perspective and which maximized the significance of religious and spiritual life.

Professor Geoghegan, as I soon found out, had begun teaching at Bowdoin in 1954, had known many of the legends of Bowdoin lore and, through his dynamic teaching style and enchanting course offerings, had become somewhat of a legend himself. He was the founder of the Bowdoin Religion Department. His typical introductory and intermediate courses included "Psychoanalysis and Religious Experience," "Existentialism," "Christianity," "Western Religious Thought," and "Myth and Mysticism" (the latter having been a freshman seminar in which Bill invited me to serve as his teaching assistant while I was a senior philosophy major). His advanced courses were unique and engaging and added much depth and scope to the Religion Department's curriculum: "The Creative Process in Abstract Painting and Religious Thought," "Comparative Mysticism," "Analytical Psychology and Religion," and "Depth-Psychology and Creativity." I took the latter seminar with him in the Spring semester of 1989.

What interested me most about Bill was that he refused to make absolute distinctions among the studies of religion, spirituality, psychology, and philosophy. In his eyes, these were all integral elements of a life-long pursuit of meaning and truth. The idea of compartmentalizing these fields of inquiry was anathema. He strove constantly to fit specific insights and lessons into the intricate fabric of "the big picture." The Jung Seminar became an arena for him to do just that. Above all, Bill's teachings have always circled around the idea and principle of *wholeness*, in terms of both philosophical speculation and everyday living.

Bill had developed the idea of the Jung Seminar in the late 1970's after having established a reading group that was composed of Bowdoin faculty members who were interested in Jung. These members included A. Leroy Greason, later to become President of the College, and Herbert R. Coursen, former Professor of English Literature. Coursen's book *The Compensatory Psyche: A Jungian Approach to Shakespeare* (University Press of America, 1986) was dedicated to Bill and the Bowdoin Jung Seminar. The original mission of that reading group was a careful line-by-line reading and discussion of Jung's revealing autobiographical memoir, *Memories, Dreams, Reflections*.

At the time when I first attended the Seminar in 1986, Bill moderated the meetings along with Brunswick-based Jungian-oriented psychotherapist, Bruce Riegel. Their shared interest in Jung's psychology had an obvious influence on the eclectic audience. The two expressed a great sense of humor while nonetheless understanding their mission at the Seminar as one of importance. Many of those who attended the Tuesday meetings, both young and old, viewed these gatherings as affairs of mind, heart, and spirit combined.

When I attended my first meeting, I was immediately struck by the feeling of having come upon a strange but wonderful little gathering in the wilderness, an enthusiastic "family" of spiritual and intellectual inquirers who were forging their own unique routes through one common forest. The message of Jungian psychology, as I was soon to find out, was a very *individual* one: each person must find his or her own "center" of existence, what Jung called *"the Self."* Jung called the pursuit of one's true Self or center *"individuation,"* the process of becoming a true individual and not merely a product of mass-minded culture. On Tuesday afternoons, the paths of these "Self-seekers" regularly and intentionally crossed as they discussed Jung's ideas about the human psyche.

But the goal of the Seminar was always a broader one than that. The study of Jung, it could be said, served as the "vehicle" or "medium" of a deeper search. These inquirers were driven to ask about *existential* matters, to ponder questions about the very meaning of their lives. These students, businesspeople, artists, and so forth had joined the Seminar to engage in a forum of mutual inquiry and ultimate spiritual concern.

As Bill himself put it succinctly in my *Orient* article "Jungian Psychology Discussed" (Oct. 10, 1986), the focus of the Seminar was "the relationship between depth-psychology and religion in a broad liberal arts context." The primary activity of the meetings at that time was *dream analysis,* where members would volunteer written records of dreams for discussion. As Bill stated in that article: "The primary activity of the Seminar is the analysis and interpretation of symbols of the Unconscious in dreams and other psychological phenomena different from, yet in terms of what, William James called 'ordinary waking consciousness.'" And to quote Dr. Riegel from the same article: "The importance [of the Seminar] is that it helps to give people a philosophy of life which we don't have, for the most part. Jungian psychology forces us to look at our own nature and how it relates to the collective."

The Jung Seminar has flourished at Bowdoin now for three decades. The independent but co-operative Bowdoin-Brunswick C. G. Jung Center for Studies in Analytical Psychology was established in part as a result of Bill Geoghegan's great enthusiasm and influence.

Bill retired from active teaching at the College over a decade ago, but he has continued to be a spirited participant in the Jung Seminar, the Jung Center, and the greater Bowdoin community. He delivered the *Fifth Mildred E. Harris Memorial Lecture* to the Jung Center on January 26, 1992. Harris had been a founding member of the Brunswick Jung Center and an active participant in the Bowdoin Jung Seminar, as well as having consulted Jung himself when the famed psychologist had visited Bailey Island, Maine in the Fall of 1936. The lecture, which served as a summary of Bill's broad interests over the preceding decade, was entitled **"The Decline of Religion and the Emergence of a New Spirituality: Nietzsche, Jung, Tillich and the Spiritual Problem of our Time."**

On March 7, 1993, Bill delivered a special lecture at the invitation of the Bangor Theological Seminary in Portland, Maine. The lecture, an extension of the Harris Lecture, was entitled **"The Essence of Spiritedness in Nietzsche, Jung, Tillich and Dürckheim: Transparence to Transcendence."** As part of a workshop hosted by William D. Geoghegan and Walter R. Christie for the Jung Center on November 30 of 1993, Bill offered a lecture entitled **"Encountering the Numinous: An Experiential Approach to Tao through Symbols of Transformation and Wholeness."** He delivered another lecture on connections between the Eastern religion of Taoism and Jungian thought for the Jung Seminar on April 4, 1995: **"Meaning and Meditation in Taoism and Jung."**

A small ceremony took place a few years ago in which Bill's office on the third floor of Massachusetts Hall, just outside the Faculty Room and occupied by him for many years, was officially dedicated to him. A handsome plaque now designates that office as "The William D. Geoghegan Room," in recognition of his many years of selfless service to Bowdoin and the Jung Seminar. In October of 1996, at the First Parish Church in Brunswick, a day-long tribute was paid to Bill by former students. At the following dinner reception Bill delivered a personal and autobiographical lecture entitled **"Spirituality as Amazing Grace."** This lecture explained the ideas of spirituality and Grace as being centered on the notions of "boundary-crossing" and "cross-fertilization." Modes of boundary-crossing in Bill's own life were exemplified in terms of friendship, collegiality, a life-long love of liberal arts learning, and marriage.

On October 16, 2001, Bill presented to the Jung Seminar a lecture entitled **"The Future of Jung's Psychology."** Bill offered here a crystallization of recent research along with his speculation that the future of Jungian psychology might well rest in the area of mind-body medicine and in the intersections among depth-psychology, spirituality, neuroscience, and quantum physics.

The above-mentioned lectures, which serve as the basis of the dialogue to follow, give only a hint of the breadth and depth of Bill Geoghegan's teachings and interests over his past four decades as an active member of the Bowdoin-Brunswick intellectual and spiritual community.

* * *

After my years of graduate studies in philosophy at Boston University, I resumed more frequent communications with Bill.   It dawned on me soon thereafter that this remarkable teacher, who had devoted himself with such selflessness to the small liberal arts classroom, had not realized the opportunity of publishing any major work during the latter half of his lengthy career.   In many ways, his magnum opus remained *Platonism in Recent Religious Thought*, the book that was based upon his very lengthy and detailed dissertation.[2] His dissertation – which traced Platonic themes in the works of such philosophers as Alfred North Whitehead and George Santayana – had been completed under the guidance of Paul Tillich, among others, while attending Union Theological Seminary and Columbia University. Bill, having also attended Yale as an undergraduate and Harvard as a graduate student, had studied under such distinguished thinkers as Reinhold Niebuhr, William Ernest Hocking, and Ernst Cassirer.   And he had devoted the remainder of his life to the teaching of philosophy and religion at Bowdoin. I knew from direct experience and not merely from his academic background that there was much that this compelling teacher could say to a contemporary audience of readers who wished to learn more about the philosophy of human spirituality, especially within the framework of Jung's psychology.

For Bill, *personal dialogue* is what philosophy is all about, which shows how deeply his Socratic and Platonic spirit runs.   Bowdoin College had provided a picturesque and traditional atmosphere in which such dialogue could flourish. And now that he was retired from full-time teaching, Bill seemed fully engaged in on-going leadership of the Jung Seminar, contemplative practice, and the quiet enjoyment of family and collegial life. He was not necessarily enthusiastic about a major publishing project, but he was full of spiritedness concerning the prospect of expanding and deepening his dialogues with others.

Bill's interests and teachings have centered upon the life-transforming spiritual insights that were the main concerns of ancient philosophers and medieval theologians and mystics, on the one hand, and contemporary existentialist writers and depth-psychologists, on the other. I had come to see many of my own philosophical interests, developed throughout graduate school and beyond, as being rooted in those ideas with which I had first become familiar in Bill's undergraduate classroom. I wanted to re-explore some of the fundamental connections that had first instilled me with a love of philosophical and spiritual learning. Certain aspects of graduate school had left me with the blasé aftertaste of the sterile rigor of *professionalized* philosophy. For me, philosophical inquiry in the Academy had begun to neglect its rootedness in the richness of spiritual life.

The shared goal of our on-going dialogue has been to *understand more clearly, with a lead from Jung's psychology, the nature of human spiritedness and self-realization, especially as they are revealed in the effort to address the contemporary problem of nihilism.* Nihilism, according to the dialogue that follows, is *the* spiritual and existential problem of our time.

But what makes this dialogue a distinctive contribution to the studies of Jungian psychology, spirituality, and nihilism? Why do we need another book on these topics when there are so many already on the library shelves? The answer, I propose, is a fairly simple one. The unique value of this conversation lies in the creative and original way in which certain ideas and thinkers have been brought together, within the overall perspective of Jungian depth-psychology, to address the problem of nihilism and to suggest possible modes of overcoming it. The dialogue expounds upon – albeit quite selectively – Bill's insights concerning the relationships among ideas from German idealist thinkers, existentialists, phenomenologists, depth-psychologists, systematic theologians, Zen masters, poets, and mystics. Given this scope and depth, along with the crafting of the connections involved and the uniquely personal form of the dialogical presentation, Bill Geoghegan and I sincerely hope that this book is not regarded simply as *yet one other* book on Jung, spirituality, and the overcoming of nihilism.

The dialogue begins, in Part One, with Bill's reflections upon **"The Essence of Spiritedness and the Emergence of a New**

Spirituality." These reflections synthesize, in an original and intriguing way, the basic ideas of Friedrich Nietzsche, Carl Gustav Jung, Paul Tillich, and Karlfried Graf Dürckheim. The latter thinker was a Bavarian Zen master and existentialist philosopher who has been overlooked in America, at least until recent years and only within small circles of scholarship. As Bill sees it, all four thinkers address the problem of nihilism and propose ways of coming to terms with it by pointing to the deeper implications of human selfhood and self-realization.

The notion of a trans-personal Self that is manifested in terms of primal, undifferentiated energy – one of the crucial conclusions of the foregoing reflections – is connected with the concepts of *numinosity* and *timelessness*. These perennial themes are also central to several Eastern philosophies. In Part Two of the dialogue, **"Exploring the Mystery of Timelessness: Jung and Lao-Tze,"** East meets West and modernity meets antiquity as Bill takes us on a tour of one of the great spiritual classics of the ancient East, Lao-tzu's *The Tao Te Ching.* In doing so, Bill outlines what he calls "the mystery of timelessness" in Jung and Lao-tzu. The discussion also serves to show how the themes of *complementarity* and *holism* lead to a spiritual ethos that is closely associated with Taoism's principle of *wei wu wei* and with Jung's principle of *active imagination.* This spiritual ethos is connected with the general notion of *meditative thinking* that is inherent in many of the world's great spiritual philosophies.

The dialogue concludes with Bill's glimpse at **"The Future of Jung's Psychology"** and his focus on the value of Jungian studies for our everyday existence and for current scholarship. Indeed, Bill has come to view *Jung's psychology as a spiritual practice and as a way of life,* as the title of our overall dialogue suggests. And as I have mentioned previously, Bill views the study of Jung's thought as especially significant now for those who are working at the cutting edge of research concerning the connections among depth-psychology, spirituality, neuroscience, mind-body medicine, and quantum physics.

In sum, Bill Geoghegan has provided us with a glimpse at one man's life of spirituality and philosophy and has also offered us a philosophy of spirituality for our own lives.

Kevin L. Stoehr, Ph.D.
Boston University
June, 2002

PART ONE

THE ESSENCE OF SPIRITEDNESS AND THE EMERGENCE OF A NEW SPIRITUALITY: ON THE SPIRITUAL PROBLEM OF OUR TIME

Introduction: Living the Questions

Kevin Stoehr: Thank you for agreeing to conduct this mutual inquiry with me, Bill.

William Geoghegan: I always enjoy visits from former students, Kevin, particularly from those who have also chosen teaching as their vocation. Thank you especially for having asked me to share this dialogue about Jung and his connection with the nature of human spirituality. Now that I have retired after forty years of teaching religion and philosophy, there has been some time to slow down and to reflect upon the various paths that have eventually converged and led me to where I am today. A chief convergence point has indeed been Jung's depth-psychology and its value in understanding spirituality.

KS: I think that many of your former students over the past forty years have gained from you a great sense of optimism. You seem to radiate it in your enthusiasm for teaching. And your teaching often revolves around the task of *finding the right questions* rather than simply finding the correct answers.

WG: Seeking the right questions lies at the heart of philosophy and religion. Perhaps you have heard the story of the young Jewish student, new to his school, who after a few weeks went up to his teacher and inquired, "Why do you rabbis always teach by asking questions?" The rabbi replied: "So what's wrong with asking questions?"

We know that there is an excellent precedent in the Western tradition for teachers to teach by asking questions: Socrates, Hillel, and Jesus come to mind immediately. At the same time, when it comes to a philosophical or religious teacher, it is not simply a matter of asking questions, but even more importantly, a matter of *living* them. The great German poet Rilke urges us to "live the questions." The following quote is taken from Rilke's *Briefe an einen jungen Dichter* or "Letters to a Young Poet," where he addresses himself to Franz Kappus:

> ...I would like to beg you, dear Sir, as well as I can, to have patience with everything unresolved in your heart and to try to love *the questions themselves* as if they were locked rooms or books written in a very foreign language. Don't search for the answers, which could not be given to you now, because you would not be able to live them. And the point is, to live everything. *Live* the questions now. Perhaps then, someday far in the future, you will gradually, without even noticing it, live your way into the answer.[1]

KS: Let's start with these poignant words, then. What have Rilke's words taught you?

WG: After having taught religion for over forty years, I have taken Rilke's maxim to heart. I have learned to live the questions and not merely to ask them and to try to answer them. This is why I regard philosophy as, fundamentally, a *spiritual practice*.

KS: Could you give me an example of a question that you have tried to live, a question that might give me a greater sense of the intellectual path that you have followed over the years?

WG: Let's see. A question that I have asked myself for some time now and with which I have been living is the following: What is *the* spiritual problem of our times? That is, what is the contemporary spiritual dilemma that all —or perhaps only most – of us must confront in order to attain happiness and the good life? And furthermore, as a part of the puzzle, who are some of the spiritual philosophers and depth-psychologists that might assist us in this confrontation? How do their ideas assist us in overcoming this spiritual problem of our age?

KS: *The* spiritual problem of our age?

WG: Yes. This problem, in my eyes anyway, is one of *nihilism.* I will come to that eventually, in much more detail. But in its essence, nihilism is the spiritual encounter with the brute *contingency* that pervades our everyday lives. Stated even more abstractly, nihilism is the human encounter with the problem of Nothingness or Non-Being – with the perishability of all things, including ourselves.

This leads us to the task of articulating the intersection of four major thinkers, among others, who have especially interested me over the course of my career – Friedrich Nietzsche, Carl Gustav Jung, Paul Tillich, and Karlfried Graf Dürckheim. You know these four thinkers, of course, Kevin.

KS: I am most familiar with Nietzsche, whom I teach frequently. He might be regarded, along with the Danish thinker Soren Kierkegaard, as one of the forefathers of existential philosophy. Your own philosophical inquiries always get back to existential questions, don't they, Bill?

WG: Yes, very much so.

KS: Paul Tillich, I know, was your former teacher. He was very much motivated by existentialist considerations in religion.

WG: Indeed. I concluded my graduate career at Columbia University and Union Theological Seminary with my dissertation, which was later published in condensed form as *Platonism in Recent Religious Thought.* One of my dissertation advisors was Tillich. He was, of course, a world-renowned philosophical theologian. His book *The Courage To Be* is, by the way, said by Harvard theologian Peter Gomes to be "the most significant book in religion published in the second half of the 20th century." [2]

KS: Jung's work has been very familiar to me ever since we studied him together in your course "Depth-Psychology and Creativity," which you offered in the Spring of 1989. As you remember, we closely studied Henri Ellenberger's *The Discovery of the Unconscious,* in which Jung's general principles and relationship to Sigmund Freud are explained. We then read Jung's autobiography *Memories, Dreams, Reflections*, which is still one of my favorite books.

WG: Yes, and one of mine too. I've read it several times. Jung was, of course, the famous Swiss psychoanalyst who broke with Freud in order to establish his own brand of study and therapy called "Analytical Psychology".

KS: I'm not familiar with Karlfried Graf Dürckheim, though.

WG: He came to my attention in later years. Dürckheim was a German-born student of Zen Buddhism, little known in the West at the time, who established a world-famous retreat in the Black Forest called "The Center for Existential Formation and Encounter."

KS: Why do you focus on these four?

WG: The short answer is that their relationship to one another has grown organically in my intellectual and emotional experience. Tillich, as I said, was one of my most esteemed teachers at Union Theological Seminary in the late 1940's and served on my dissertation committee. I found Jung useful when I began teaching comparative religion over forty years ago, especially his concepts of the Collective Unconscious and its archetypes and, even more importantly, his notion of the individuation process as the differentiation and re-integration of the ego and the Self. It was necessary to consider Nietzsche in teaching Existentialism over the years. Later I was to learn of his enormous and generally unknown or unconsidered influence on Jung.

KS: And you regard these four thinkers as having addressed the same general problem?

WG: Yes. In my view Nietzsche raised *the* philosophical problem for the twentieth century, but by no means resolved it. Jung addressed the same problem *psychologically* and resolved it satisfactorily in that way for himself and for many others. Tillich addressed and resolved the problem *theologically* for many.
  Nevertheless, up until this point, I felt something was missing in my exploration of this problem, what Jung calls "the missing fourth." I found an actual and symbolic "fourth" in Dürckheim, whose thought

builds upon his three predecessors and extends their ideas in terms of a comprehensive emphasis upon the *experiential*, the *self-transformational* and the *methodological* in philosophy, psychology, religion, and theology.   One of the chief themes of Dürckheim's thought – that of *self-realization* or *Selbstverwirklichung* – is indeed the unifying thread in this diverse quartet of thinkers. As Jung proclaims in the very first sentence to the Prologue of his autobiography: "My life is a story of the self-realization of the Unconscious."[3]

So what I'd really like to discuss with you, as an overall theme, is the concept of *self-realization in relation to the spiritual problem of nihilism*. And the articulation of that theme certainly involves a few other crucial concepts along the way.

I want to discuss the decline of religion and the emergence of a new spirituality in the light of these four thinkers. The notion of a religious decline and a new spiritual emergence could be applied to a substantial series of phenomena in any of the major cultures that I know anything about, from the ancient Chinese right through the Greek and the Roman, and so forth, up to the present. An old form of religion is always being superseded by a new form of religion or spirituality. So I will turn more directly to the issues involved with the spiritual problem of our time and how these issues are interpreted and addressed by these four strikingly provocative thinkers.

I view these spiritual philosophers as representing a climax to the development of Western religious thought from the late Renaissance to the near-present. Nietzsche seems paradoxically to combine the *decline of religion* at its lowest point – symbolized by his famous, if quite unoriginal, assertion of the "death of God" – and the emergence (for better or worse) of a *new, powerful, and open-ended spirituality*. Jung enters the picture because he had profound affinities with Nietzsche: he knew Nietzsche's masterwork, *Also Sprach Zarathustra*, marvelously well, and at the same time he was able to provide a very extensive and incisive psychological critique of Nietzsche. Tillich and Dürckheim assist us in framing and developing the discussion of Nietzsche and Jung, especially as they synthesize the common existential, religious, and psychological issues in their unique ways.

KS: What do you mean by a "new spirituality?"

WG: I would propose, in a preliminary way, that this "new spirituality" – which emerged in the later part of the 20th century (and which has actually been emerging since the first prominent signals of change were uttered by Nietzsche toward the end of the 19th century) – is centered around the notion of *spiritedness*. I suggest that these four thinkers provide invaluable conceptual resources to assist us in explaining the contemporary decline of religion and the emergence of a new spirituality, especially as that newer spirituality revolves around the central idea of the *spiritedness of self-realization*.

KS: Why do you use the term "spiritedness"?

WG: I offer the word "spiritedness" in connection with self-realization because it connotes, especially through the German form of that term, a better sense of what all four thinkers are driving at: *Feuer*, or fire; *Mut*, or courage; *Lebendigkeit*, or liveliness; and *Energie*, or energy. All of these terms have connotations of fervor, passion, and mettle that are best associated with the term "spiritedness." Spiritedness conveys a sense of the *absolutely unconditional concern* – the passion – with which each person should address the question of *Non-Being*, that enigmatic concept which lies at the heart of Western humanity's great spiritual problem.

Spiritedness especially suggests the sense of power or *Macht* in Nietzsche's famous concept of *the Will to Power* (*der Wille zur Macht*). It is captured in the title of Tillich's famous Terry Lectures at Yale, *The Courage to Be* (*Der Mut zum Sein*). Dürckheim, as we shall see, also gives this concept of spiritedness a radical personal development. And the term connotes the heroic fortitude that Jung had to summon in order to survive his famous "Confrontation with the Unconscious," as expressed in *Memories, Dreams, Reflections*. Spiritedness expresses the chief characteristic of those who have embarked upon and realized to a significant degree that path of self-realization which Jung calls "individuation."

Self-Realization and the Influence of Hegel

KS: Much of your teaching in your later years focused on this notion of *individuation*.

WG: Yes. Individuation, or becoming whole as a unique person, is the core concept of Jung's psychology. At the very beginning of his autobiography, Jung uses the term *"Selbstverwirklichung"* or *"self-realization"* as a synonym for *individuation*. So then we might ask ourselves: What do these two Latinized abstractions really mean?

What they mean can be garnered from the end of Jung's autobiography, where he says, in effect, that all he had done in his nearly eighty-six years is to have lived his life on the basis of something unknown and greater than himself.[4] Individuation means a *lived* life as distinct from what Jung calls a "provisional" life.[5] We might recall here Rilke's motto that urges us to "live the questions." Jung was a man and a thinker who certainly lived his questions, and these questions always pointed to a deeper conception of experiential reality and therefore to some higher form of self-knowledge.

One of the things that I like best about Jung is his distinction between a neurosis, which is an inhibiting of life-function, and a "pseudo-neurosis", which has nothing to do with any clinical aspect of one's personality but has everything to do with a lack of a sense of meaning, purpose, direction, or orientation in one's life.[6]

KS: I know that Viktor Frankl's notion of *logo-therapy*, expressed clearly in his book *Man's Search for Meaning*, is directed toward such a deficiency of spiritedness and self-realization.

WG: Yes, that's a wonderful book. Frankl discusses his own process of self-realization in terms of his struggles to cope with the horrifying experiences of the concentration camp.

KS: What do we mean when we call a person "self-realized"?

WG: It appears to me that one who is self-realized or who has undertaken a personal path of individuation may be said to have gained a perspective on his or her life which is both self-liberating and self-enlightening. Liberation seems to occur in terms of a gradual freeing of one's attention from provisional or transient interests to what Tillich called "ultimate" or "infinite" concern. I think here of Socrates' famous imperative, taken from the Delphic maxim: "Know thyself."

KS: Jung's small and wonderful text *The Undiscovered Self*, which I have taught before, takes as its primary theme that of self-knowledge.

WG: Yes, it is a central theme in his overall thinking. Enlightenment is constituted by a search for self-knowledge, taking one beyond the mere confines of the ego-personality and providing a richer and more meaningful definition of one's psyche and personal identity. I think here of a Sanskrit term that is often applied to the greatest adepts in Indian spirituality, like Gautama Buddha or Mahavira, the founder of Jainism: *Jivan-mukta*, "being liberated while still alive." This quality is characteristic of those who have achieved a significant measure of self-realization or individuation.

KS: The notion of self-realization seems to have been present in nearly all cultures since time immemorial.

WG: The idea of self-realization has a long history going back four millennia, and yet it has a timeless pertinence. It is not to be confused with ego-development or the cultivation of self-esteem. Although it includes psychological and sociological dimensions, it is basically a philosophical, religious, and spiritual concept. Rather than taking the time to sketch the history of this concept, I wish to view its recent development to date.

A clue is given by the French phenomenologist Maurice Merleau-Ponty, writing in 1964: "All of the great philosophical ideas of the past century – the philosophies of Marx and Nietzsche, phenomenology, German existentialism, and psychoanalysis – had their beginnings in Hegel."[7] Hegel gives us perhaps the grandest and most intricate conception of self-realization in the history of Western philosophy. And he relates this concept of self-realization directly to his concept of Spirit or *Geist*. A few general remarks on the philosophy of Hegel will serve as a good introduction to the four thinkers upon whom I want to focus. Hegel focused his intellectual energies upon the very structure of *mind* as well as *spirit* – these being identical for him, what he called "*Geist*."

Hegel developed a detailed philosophical system that revolves around the unifying method of Dialectic. Dialectic is a processual method of reasoning that is constituted through the recognition of contradictions. Occasioned by such recognition, and through the rational desire to seek higher and richer levels of thought whereby these contradictions are overcome, the goal of *integrated wholeness* emerges. Hegel's Dialectic overcomes dichotomies by unifying and integrating opposites. And you did your dissertation on Hegelian Logic, Kevin. Would you agree with that assessment?

KS: Yes. Your emphasis on the integration of opposites here seems crucial to me. We learn at the very beginning of Hegel's famous *Science of Logic* that it is contradictory to say that the concept of *Being* (what we might call the idea of "*is*-ness") is identical to the concept of *Nothingness*, since they are opposites. We cannot say that something *is* and *is not* at the same time and in the same degree. However, since both concepts refer to complete indeterminacy, they are equally empty and without definite content. The two ideas tell us about *nothing in particular*. So these two concepts are opposites that are nonetheless somehow also the same. This is the contradiction that must be overcome. And Hegel does overcome the contradiction by positing a new concept, that of *Becoming*, which integrates both Being and Nothingness in order to make sense of itself. That is, in order to say that something *becomes* something else, we have to say that it *ceases to be* one type of thing and that it *begins to be* another type of thing. So through this new concept of Becoming, we have overcome the contradiction in saying that the concepts of Being and Nothingness are actually the same. The idea of Becoming allows us to say that something *both is and is not*, but only in different respects and according to some kind of change.

WG: Becoming, in fact, is the most abstract form of what we might call integrated wholeness. In its most basic aspect, self-realization is a *process of becoming*, an act of self-transformation.

As a beginning point, then, I would like to adopt Hegel's notion of self-realization as that of a transformational search for integrated wholeness. In more philosophical terminology, we might call such integrated wholeness a "synthetic unity of opposites," like the unification of the ideas of Being and Nothingness at the beginning of Hegel's Logic.

I believe, then, that the speculative and systematic essence of Hegel's difficult philosophy can be stated in his own five words from the Preface to his famous *Phenomenology of Spirit*: "The truth is the whole" ("*Das Wahre ist das Ganze.*").[8] Religious knowledge helps us to attain this insight through the equation of truth and integrated wholeness.

KS: Hegel intrigues me, for one reason, because he maintains so vehemently that Christianity is the highest form of religion.   That would be a rather risky belief to hold today in our contemporary turn to more multicultural modes of thinking.

WG: Yes, and why does Hegel maintain this claim about Christianity? It has to do with his dialectical method, does it not?   And this topic perhaps helps us to understand more clearly why religion in its older, institutional forms has declined in recent times and why a new spirituality that focuses upon integrated wholeness is emerging. Hegel's dialectical method and his comparative study of world religions might serve as a guiding thread in speculating about the transition from an old religion to a new spirituality.

KS: I know that Christianity for Hegel reveals, more explicitly than other religions, the dialectical principle of the rational order of Spirit or *Geist*. "The truth is the whole" because Truth is expressed in its most explicit form by a philosophy that accomplishes both the *complete self-realization* of human thought as well as the *complete self-realization* of divine thought.   So Hegel proposes the goal of self-realization as integrated wholeness on a grand, even cosmic, scale.

Hegel's notion of self-realization as systematic wholeness expresses the coincidence of both human and divine self-knowledge. Hegel's formulation of dialectical idealism in these terms established a defense of Christianity as the most enlightened mode of *religious* self-realization.   And yet, according to Hegel, it is *philosophy* and not *lived religion* that affords the genuine pinnacle of self-realization.   Even though Hegel was a very religious philosopher, a "philosopher of Spirit," he still maintains that Religion (along with Art) ranks *below* Philosophy as a mode of expressing what he calls "*Geist*" or "Spirit."

WG: Well, the fact that Hegel had prioritized speculative philosophy over *lived* religion – even over the lived practice of the *Christian* religion – was a clear signal that religion had become ripe for criticism and analysis.   Institutional Christianity, for example, began to be questioned by radical and existentially motivated philosophers such as Soren Kierkegaard, who criticized the Danish Lutheran Church for not being authentically Christian in the genuinely spiritual sense of that religion. The road was now open for those radical critics of religion like Ludwig Feuerbach and Karl Marx and Friedrich Nietzsche. You see, here was the decline and apparent death-rattle of a Christianity which once provided a sense of "the meaning of the Whole" for Western civilization. Christianity, and Western religion overall, became intellectualized and overly conceptualized. Religion was, in many quarters, no longer *lived*. I think that it was this decline which, in the last half of the nineteenth century, prompted Nietzsche to accelerate the demise of institutional Christianity as he knew it in order that his own new myth of the meaning of "the whole" might emerge. However, even though Hegel may well have assisted in the decline of official Christendom through his over-emphasis on religious rationalism, it was his notion of self-realization as integrated wholeness that carried over implicitly to the newer forms of emerging spirituality.

We see here an obvious and profound example of the decline of one form of institutionalized religion and the emergence of a new, personalized form of spiritual self-realization. And as I had mentioned before, Nietzsche is the philosopher who first fully captured the character of such a transition.

The Spiritual Problem of our Age: Nietzsche and Nihilism

KS: Let me ask you to take a step back before we delve into the teachings of Nietzsche. You mentioned earlier *"the* spiritual problem of our age" as one of nihilism. What is this problem, and how does it relate to the notions of self-realization and individuation?

WG: I would like to define in a preliminary sense the spiritual problem of our age as an *incubating nihilism*. And I would characterize this brooding nihilism in a graphic way with a stanza from the beginning of William Butler Yeats's famous poem "The Second Coming," published in 1921. The words are hauntingly familiar and compelling in their autonomous power. They seem to live in the mind long after you hear or read them for the first time, and they seem constantly to be confirmed by recurring and current events. Yeats wrote:

> Things fall apart; the center cannot hold;
> Mere anarchy is loosed upon the world,
> The blood-dimmed tide is loosed, and everywhere
> The ceremony of innocence is drowned;
> The best lack all conviction, while the worst
> Are full of passionate intensity.[9]

KS: That's pretty nihilistic.

WG: Yes. This poem helps to give a sense of nihilism as *the* spiritual problem that is recognized and addressed by all four of the chief thinkers whom I have mentioned – Nietzsche, Jung, Tillich, and Karlfried Graf Dürckheim. As I interpret these four thinkers, this spiritual problem is at bottom a brooding, seething, sometimes violently erupting nihilism, both inner and outer, usually masked by all sorts of cultural and personal distractions and self-deceptions, to such an extent that we have become habituated to it. Nihilism has become banalized to such an extent that it is no longer recognized for what it is. And so my central theme is that the spiritedness of self-realization is the response of these four thinkers to nihilism.

KS: From my own studies of existentialist philosophy and literature, I would agree with you that nihilism is not simply a rejection of conventional and traditional values, although it is often defined that way. Nihilism, as you mentioned earlier, is a fundamental recognition of the fact that our lives are fleeting and perishable – pervaded by the presence of Non-Being or Nothingness. Due to that recognition, we soon find that we have lost any hope of stability or permanence that might be provided by traditional values and beliefs or by a given social or political system. We are faced with the contingencies of existence in which there are no absolute guarantees and no unconditional sources of salvation or redemption.

WG: Yes. In fact, Nietzsche described himself as "the perfect nihilist" in the sense that he had lived through a confrontation with the "reality" of Nothingness, had personally experienced it, and was somehow transformed in the process, so as to overcome it. This experience of addressing directly the presence of Non-Being, and the proposal to overcome it through self-realization, is the theme of Nietzsche's masterwork, *Thus Spake Zarathustra*.

There does not exist in any sense a definitive interpretation of Nietzsche. Estimates range from the one extreme of regarding him as an exemplar of the Christian spirituality of the future to the other extreme of interpreting his thought as a demonic parody of the tradition of which he was the product. My concern with his thought nowadays is primarily its influence upon Jung, as well as its more general importance for Tillich and Dürckheim in having made thematic the basic cultural presupposition of the so-called "post-modern" or "futurist" period in which we are said to live. This presupposition is, of course, the emergence of nihilism as a destructive cultural and philosophical attitude.

KS: Do you see a direct connection between Nietzsche's personal and cultural background, on the one hand, and this "basic cultural presupposition" or "attitude," on the other?

WG: I do. Nietzsche was born in 1844 and died in 1900. The year of his death was a symbolic one in that it marked not only the end of the century but also perhaps the end of an age. There was a widespread sense that the Christian era was drawing to a close – especially, as Tillich points out, the Protestant era. Although Tillich contends that the Protestant *principle* is eternal and universal – it is seen at work in the Hebrew prophets, for example – the Protestant *era*, as a schematized, formalized organization of numinous energy, was coming to an end.[10] I'll elaborate upon this concept of numinosity and the numinous a bit later.

Protestantism, as it had been known in the West since the time of Luther (with his cardinal expression of its essence as "justification by faith"), had degenerated into the culture-Protestantism which Kierkegaard earlier in the nineteenth century had called "Christendom" in order to distinguish it from genuine Christianity. It was into this milieu that Nietzsche, with as many as fifteen Lutheran parsons altogether on his family tree, entered upon his iconoclastic prophetic mission.

KS: Nietzsche had distinguished himself early on as an intellectual prodigy, had he not?

WG: Nietzsche was a brilliant young man. At the age of twenty-four he became Professor of Classical Philology at the University of Basel, a virtually unprecedented achievement. He became ill shortly thereafter, received a pension from the University and spent the rest of his life as a lonely wanderer in northern Italy, southern Switzerland, and the south of France, writing a great deal. His collected works number fifteen volumes.

KS: And you regard *Thus Spake Zarathustra* as Nietzsche's most important work?

WG: I do. It is a grand myth that teaches us how to overcome the spiritual problem of our contemporary humanity. Nietzsche was certainly ahead of his time and viewed his philosophy as one of the future. In the mid-1880's he wrote *Zarathustra*, although some notable works preceded and immediately followed it. Zarathustra was modeled after the Iranian prophet, Zoroaster (as he was known among the Greeks), who lived around 600 BC. Zoroaster is the archetypal prophet of what theologians call an "apocalyptic eschatology," that form of intensely-charged imaginal discourse which purports to disclose last or ultimate things (and in view of their transcendent importance, one could just as well say "first things").

This is exactly what Nietzsche had in mind. He wished to disclose first, last, and ultimate things. Shortly after writing his masterwork, Nietzsche's health began to deteriorate at a precipitous rate – physically, emotionally, and mentally. He was beginning, for example, to sign his letters "Dionysus" or "The Crucified." Finally he became paralyzed by psychosis and spent the last decade of his life in silent solitude.

KS: How have you approached Nietzsche when teaching about his revolutionary ideas?

WG: I deal with Nietzsche in a three-fold way: as a *philosopher*, a *psychologist*, and a *numinous personality*. The essential matter which Nietzsche addresses in his three-fold manner is, as we have already remarked, nihilism, the contemporary expression of what Tillich later calls the human condition of "tragic and universal self-estrangement."[11] Nietzsche's feeling for nihilism has a classical, Biblical, archetypal strength. He illustrates it with a quotation from Silenos, a companion of Dionysus: "What is best is utterly beyond man's reach: Not to be born, not to *be*, to be *nothing*." And Nietzsche then adds, if I remember correctly: "The second best for you is to die soon."

Nietzsche called himself "the perfect nihilist," as I had mentioned, because he believed that he had successfully passed through that dark night of the soul in terms of an experiential self-transformation. He had passed through nihilism, overcome it, and achieved, to use his own word, "redemption" (*Genesung*, from the German verb *genesen*, to come through alive, to be delivered, to come joyfully home).[12] He describes this conversion of selfhood and existence in his intellectual and spiritual autobiography, *Ecce Homo*. There he speaks of the origin of his masterpiece *Zarathustra* in terms that might very well describe the inspiration of an Old Testament prophet by an unknown God. His "ultimate concern", to use Tillich's term for an unconditional and infinite interest, was to proclaim the gospel of the overcoming of nihilism, and *Zarathustra* is this gospel.

KS: So how do you bring together the themes of nihilism and self-realization when dealing with Nietzsche?

WG: The general and essential point to be made here is that the overcoming of nihilism is to be accomplished through "self-realization." Nietzsche takes his cue from Pindar's maxim, "Become what you are." The subtitle of his autobiographical work *Ecce Homo* is "How One Becomes What One Is."[13]

KS: How do you understand that maxim? I've always found it to be a fascinating one. The German philosopher Martin Heidegger, I know, adopts it and refers to it briefly in his major early work *Being and Time*.[14]

WG: Yes, and Heidegger, as we know, was enormously influenced by Nietzsche, as was Jung. The term "become" implies total, complete, radical, experiential self-transformation. The phrase "what you are" implies what Nietzsche, and later Jung, was to call the "Self" (*Selbst*) – literally, "the itself", recalling the "thing-in-itself" or "the Absolute" in the philosophies of Kant and Hegel. This "itself" is "what you are" (i.e., "the Self"), referring to your full psychological and spiritual potential as an individual.

Let's now examine this notion of our individuating task of self-realization more closely, in reference both to Nietzsche's philosophy and to Nietzsche himself. Let's talk about Nietzsche and his philosophy according to the first mode of my three-fold schema for understanding him: Nietzsche as a philosopher.

Nietzsche as Philosopher

KS: How did Nietzsche view himself in terms of the history of Western or European-centered philosophy?

WG: Nietzsche regarded himself primarily as a philosopher, as the greatest since Plato, with respect to whom even Kant and Hegel were but "philosophical laborers", as he calls them, "noble exemplars." In addition, Nietzsche had a very high opinion of the vocation of philosophy, which Plato in fact exemplified because he was the true founder of Western civilization through his "rational optimism."

Such optimism Plato learned from his teacher, Socrates, who taught and reiterated endlessly that "virtue is knowledge" and that one's primary task is to examine one's life and thereby to gain self-knowledge, as Plato informs us in his famous dialogue *The Apology*. This type of philosophical optimism derives from the belief that man's rational mind, following the principle of causality, could penetrate the deepest abysses of the unknown. This was Plato's great contribution and it was eventually carried forth to constitute the foundation of Western civilization by means of what Nietzsche calls "Platonism for the people."

KS: Let's discuss that phrase "Platonism for the people," if you would.

WG: It gets to the heart of Nietzsche's critique of Western culture, of course. "Platonism for the people" consists of two basic forms, the Christian religion and modern science. These are the two cultural embodiments of Socratic-Platonic optimism. "Platonism for the people" is founded, says Nietzsche, on the basic principle of the *will to truth*. But the will to truth, alas, was tragically flawed. It was tragically flawed because it was based on the "spirit of revenge" or *resentment*.

Platonism, Christianity, and science (along with technology) wish to correct *Nature* which, taken in its broadest sense, is simply that which exists. They take *vengeance* upon Nature, to make it better than it is. This is a slightly different form of resentment than the type expressed by slave-type personalities in their envious reaction against master-type personalities, as Nietzsche also taught us. But for Nietzsche, Nature was the absolute. There is nothing above or beyond it. As Zarathustra says, "There is no outside," meaning nothing outside of the "Whole" which we experience and call "Nature."[15]   We are encapsulated by a Nature of which Nietzsche has a most generous concept. But it is this spirit of revenge and the will to truth, he contends, which produced the "death of God" and therefore the nihilism of his day. Due to this spirit and will, everything becomes merely a passive and intellectualized object for humans, even Nature and God.

KS: So this cultural legacy of Platonism has, in some way, brought about the spiritual problem of our times?

WG: This is the case, according to Nietzsche. His basic critical contention is that Platonism and Christianity have, ironically, created the cultural crisis of nihilism through their "will to truth" and rational optimism. Under the assault of the "will to truth," first went Christian dogma, then Christian morality, then the importance of lived religion. Then went the essential fabric of the civilization founded upon them. We are then left with the *nihil*, or nothing.

KS: So we return to the problem of Nothingness or Non-Being.

WG: Yes. Nihilism, by its very name and nature, implies the problem of Non-Being, as we have mentioned.

KS: So Platonism and Christianity and science, born of rational optimism, have led us to our current nihilistic condition. What is to be done about this?

WG: According to Nietzsche, there must be a "transvaluation of all values," a complete revolution in value-thinking, and the will to truth must be overturned by another will, another primal striving, which Nietzsche derives from his forebear, the German philosopher Arthur Schopenhauer. Schopenhauer's great work *The World as Will and Representation* is a refutation of that rational optimism that was the legacy of ancient Greek philosophy and the Age of Enlightenment.

According to Nietzsche, this primordial principle of striving is the "Will to Power" (*Der Wille zur Macht*). As Nietzsche says, "This world is the will to power – and nothing besides!"[16] His notion of the Will to Power bears a remarkable resemblance to German theologian Rudolf Otto's concept of *the numinous*, although Otto's book on numinosity, entitled *Das Heilige* or *The Idea of the Holy*, appeared nearly two decades after Nietzsche died. We will return to Otto. The Will to Power is a non-rational, numinous, undifferentiated energy rooted fundamentally in the physical. It is described variously by Nietzsche as the will to dominate, to master, to overcome, and above all to overcome oneself (or self-transcend) by rising above the spirit of envy, vindictiveness, and revenge. Countering that complex spiritual pathology that he calls *ressentiment* or "resentment" is the Will to Power supremely expressed, as the will to create "by letting things be and become."

"To let things be and become" is a good way of expressing Nietzsche's synthesis of the *being and becoming* of an individual. Laurence Lampert, in his excellent book *Nietzsche's Teaching: An Interpretation of Thus Spoke Zarathustra*, refers also to this rather Heideggerian idea of "letting beings be," which means to allow things to become what they truly are[17]. One must accept one's existence or being in terms of one's own becoming or self-transformation.

KS: This is Nietzsche's emphasis on the Will to Power as a principle of self-overcoming or self-transcendence. Is this where he arrives at his idea of "the eternal return"?

WG: Yes. Co-equal with this primordial, revolutionary, creative Will to Power is Nietzsche's concept of the "Eternal Recurrence of the Same" (*die ewige Wiederkehr des Gleichen*), Nietzsche's fundamental teaching and the centerpiece of *Zarathustra*. Basically "eternal recurrence" means the universalization and absolutization of self-realization – namely, "Become what you (nothing excluded) are."

KS: I've always found this principle of the eternal return to be one of the most intriguing *and* frustrating in my study of philosophy. I'm never quite sure whether we should understand it as a metaphysical or a psychological principle.

WG: Well, the notion of eternal recurrence, I have found, can best be summarized in relation to three direct maxims or propositions or attitudes. Let me go through them:

Nietzsche adopts the Latin maxim "*Amor fati*," meaning love of fate or destiny, hearkening back to the philosophies of such Stoic thinkers as Epictetus and Marcus Aurelius.[18] One must identify with one's destiny and unite with it. One must accept one's past, no matter how repugnant.[19] This can be illustrated in part by the contemporary psycho-therapeutic doctrine of self-acceptance, but for Nietzsche it is truly philosophical, conveying the sense of a vocational mission of universal significance, akin to that of a Socrates, a Jeremiah, a Dionysus, or a Christ.

Zarathustra's culminating understanding of the principle of the eternal recurrence might be best expressed by the maxim that declares: "This life, thine eternal life."[20] This is an expression unifying the opposites of time and eternity, and thus repudiating the split between the so-called "this world" of insignificant transitoriness and an "other world" of transcendent permanence.

The proposition in which Nietzsche expresses eternal recurrence is perhaps his most deeply significant statement, articulated by his alter ego Zarathustra : "But thus I willed it."[21] This imperative signifies a complete acceptance of one's past, no matter how miserable and regretful the past may appear to one from a present perspective, and therefore it signifies complete self-acceptance and self-realization. Nietzsche's problem was how to will whole-heartedly what he found totally repugnant.   He has many expressions for that element of repugnancy in human experience, of *"tremendum"* or repulsion, which he calls collectively "the shadow" (*der Schatten*).[22]   Jung was later to define the shadow as a psychological phenomenon, as that essential part of our personal reality which is nevertheless rejected by us and which somehow needs to be reintegrated – "re-cognized" – if we are to live out of a vital wholeness.   Nietzsche regards the "most contemptible" thing as the "last man," someone who is a banal, trivial, complacent, herd-minded, unconscious, bourgeois nihilist.[23]

KS: So we should acknowledge what is most contemptible in order to overcome it.

WG: Right.   And the primacy of an absolute or unconditional personal Will with unlimited trans-personal implications is *the* key to self-realization, to *becoming* what one at bottom *is*.   The crucial test of the Will to Power is the willingness to "let be and become" the last man. Acknowledging in some decisive sense his identity with that which he most despised was the necessary prelude to the advent of the Superman or Overman (*der Übermensch*).   This ideal personality-type signifies humanity as such in its own self-transcendence.

KS: So it would appear that this self-transcending character of the Will to Power must be grasped primarily in *psychological* terms.

WG: As I understand it, this primal striving eventually necessitates a recognition of the individual's personality as a complex of mainly unconscious drives and instincts which are represented to human consciousness in symbolic, and often deceptive, forms of expression. Therefore, I'll turn now to a view of Nietzsche as psychologist and then as a numinous personality. That will require a detailed explanation of the concept of numinosity, which I have mentioned earlier.

Nietzsche as Psychologist and as Numinous Personality

KS: How does Nietzsche fit into the history of psychology and dynamic psychiatry? I remember your once talking about Nietzsche's tremendous influence upon Freud and Jung.

WG: Well, as Ellenberger points out in his *The Discovery of the Unconscious*, Nietzsche is regarded by qualified observers as the true founder of modern depth-psychology, the psychology of the Unconscious as formulated most explicitly by Freud and Jung. This is implicitly acknowledged by Freud and openly admitted by Jung. One of America's leading Jungian analysts, teachers, and scholars, Edward F. Edinger, contended that Nietzsche, not Freud or Jung, was "the first depth-psychologist," that he was a "heroic martyr" of depth-psychology, and that his life was a "noble tragedy" and "heroic sacrifice."

Even as Nietzsche was writing in his later years, depth-psychology was being developed as a science in Europe, notably by Freud. Now Freud, when he published *The Interpretation of Dreams* in 1900, possessed the works of Nietzsche but refused to read them because he was afraid that his own "scientific" approach, as he understood it, would be contaminated by Nietzsche's philosophical "speculations." Nevertheless, he later used the word "astonishing" to characterize the congruence between Nietzsche's teachings and his own.   Furthermore, many, if not most, of Jung's basic ideas were anticipated by Nietzsche, and he is deeply indebted to him in a positive sense. At the same time Nietzsche's manifest irrationality and ultimate fate raised serious questions for Jung, as we shall see.

KS: I remember you saying once that Nietzsche is actually a very Socratic thinker, despite his critique of Platonism. I would certainly agree with that, especially in terms of their emphases on self-knowledge.

WG: Nietzsche takes his lead from Socrates' pursuit of self-knowledge while rejecting his and Plato's over-emphasis on rational optimism.   Nietzsche aims at reviving the "ancient and venerable hypothesis of soul" because psychology in that deeper sense of the term, as a study or rational account of the soul, is the pathway toward answers to fundamental problems – i.e., problems of philosophy, of religion, and of ultimate concern. Socrates taught that the psyche and its "tendance" is the primary responsibility of a human being. Beyond Socrates, Nietzsche says, there is only one psychologist from whom he was able to learn anything worth learning: the deeply intuitive Russian novelist Fyodor Dostoevsky.

KS: With all of that said, what is the *essence* of Nietzsche's psychological teaching?

WG: This teaching may be summarized as follows. What is ordinarily regarded as an individual, or undivided, human personality is in reality a cluster of sub-personalities: autonomous, affect-laden representations of physiological drives and instincts engendered by the primal undifferentiated energy of the Will to Power. The decisive aspect of this concept of the human psyche is that the true center of the personality is not the conscious, rational ego, but what Nietzsche calls the Self (*das Selbst*), a timeless, self-identical "this is I." For Nietzsche, the Self, rooted in the body, is a natural, unconscious, regulative principle, the ground and true center of the human personality.[24] And above all, this "Self" is a self-creative organization of those drives and instincts which often emerge into conscious life in a deceptive, disguised, sometimes destructive manner. Thus Nietzsche anticipates Freud's major claim that man (that is, man's *ego*) is not "master in his own house."

   The portrait of self-transcendence and self-realization that is undertaken in Nietzsche's *Zarathustra* gives us a detailed sense of this thinker's criticism of the ego's limitations and his espousal of the numinous energies of the Self or Will to Power. And yet it is the portrait of Nietzsche himself as a numinous personality that affords us our most telling glimpse of the glories and dangers of such a process of creative self-discovery. The concept of the multi-dimensional psyche leads us to such a view of Nietzsche.

KS: You refer to Nietzsche as a "numinous personality." What does that mean exactly?

WG: The aptness of the designation of "numinous personality" is shown by comparing Rudolf Otto's view of the numinous with Nietzsche's account of the origin of *Zarathustra*. Before turning to

Nietzsche's depiction of the inspiration that infused his masterwork, I will explain briefly what Otto meant by the terms "numinosity" and "the numinous".

Rudolf Otto was a colleague of Tillich at Marburg University. In his day Otto was an outstanding scholar of comparative religion and visited Africa, the Near East, India particularly, also China, and instituted one of the first museums of comparative religion in the Western world, at Marburg. Otto's book *Das Heilige* (1917), translated as *The Idea of the Holy*, is one of the few really seminal works, in my opinion, in twentieth century philosophy of religion or philosophical theology.

Numinosity is a profound example of a phenomenon that can only be explained as a coincidence of opposites or *coincidentia oppositorum*. This principle, I think, is a perennial one throughout the history of philosophy and religion.

KS: We have already seen the notion of a coincidence of opposites when we remarked upon Hegel's dialectical method of overcoming contradictions – conflicts or divisions between opposing propositions.

WG: Right. Numinosity involves this idea of the integration of opposites. In Otto's view, the numinous is the integration of the *rational* and the *irrational* in terms of religious and spiritual experience.

Otto's basic concept is that religion itself is a coincidence of opposites, of non-rational and rational elements. *The Idea of the Holy* was sub-titled "An Inquiry into the non-rational factor in the idea of the divine and its relation to the rational." Otto says that he wrote the book (and many would agree with him) because the rational element in religion had been over-emphasized ever since the time of Kant and Hegel. This over-emphasis became apparent when Christian theology attempted to adapt itself to the turbulent currents and ferments of the 19th and early 20th centuries.

KS: Why does Otto use the term "numinous?"

WG: The name that Otto gives to the non-rational element of religion is the "numinous" or *numinosum*. This term is derived from the Latin *numen*, which means "spirit" in an undifferentiated sense. By the "numinous" Otto means a kind of universally diffused, undifferentiated energy, akin to the *mana* and other forms of universal energy that anthropologists had discovered in many primal religions all over the world. The implication of primal energy here relates conspicuously, as I have suggested, to Nietzsche's notion of primal selfhood or Self as founded upon the Will to Power.

KS: So what is the essence of numinous experience?

WG: It is the encounter with the awesome as an objective, yet not necessarily material, reality. The way in which you know that you are experiencing that which is objectively awesome is by means of the *feeling*, the immediate awareness (*das Gefühl*) of the awesome as *Other*. That is to say, the feeling of awe is not merely subjective, but is the recognition of that which is objectively awesome. A thunderbolt, for example, would be an excellent example for that which is awesome, and the feeling that it induces in the experiencing of the awesome is, as Otto says, "creature-feeling" or "creature-consciousness."[25]

KS: I can see why you view this notion of numinosity as a central one in your studies of religion and depth-psychology.

WG: Yes, and it was more than just *a* central concept for Otto. The numinous, Otto claims, is the original substance of religion. And that which is rational in religion – theology, the moral code, the entire symbolic system – consists of "schematizations," formulations or humanizations, of this primal undifferentiated energy. Otto equates the numinous with the notion of a tremendous and overpowering and fascinating mystery. He uses the Latin phrase *"mysterium tremendum"* and adds the Latin adjectives *"fascinans"* and *"majestas."*[26]   By mystery or *mysterium* he means that the underived substance of religion is in and of itself incomprehensible and inexpressible.   It is experienced, however, in a two-fold manner, in terms of a fundamental tension: the opposition of the experience of *tremendum*, of that which repels, upsets, and shakes up, and the experience of *fascinans*, of that which attracts magnetically, hypnotically, irresistibly.

KS: A coincidence of opposites.

WG: Precisely. The effort to come to rational, moral terms with the non-rational, amoral, ambivalent, awesome numinous is of the essence of what man knows as religion, particularly Western religion, and especially Biblical religion. For example, the primordial numinous experience of being torn – caught ambivalently between the repulsion of the awesome numinous on the one hand and being magnetically attracted toward it on the other – gets schematized in the Biblical sense in the following way. The *tremendum* gets schematized as divine wrath and the *fascinans* as divine grace, so that Otto defines divine love in the Biblical sense as "quenched wrath," a unity of opposites.[27]

KS: Could you give a Biblical example of this?

WG: The best developed example that Otto gives, and I think the best that can be given, is the story of Job, where the numinous is expressed in the voice out of the whirlwind and creature-consciousness is expressed by Job's responses to that awesome manifestation of divine power.[28] The story ends with reconciliation between the awesome and incomprehensible power and wisdom of Deity, on the one hand, and the limited, but nonetheless impressive, moral and rational integrity of Man, on the other. Once again, we arrive at a coincidence of opposites, a coincidence that is manifested in terms of numinous experience.

KS: So how can we relate the notion of the numinous back to Nietzsche?

WG: The power of the numinous is evident in what Nietzsche wrote in his literary autobiography, *Ecce Homo*, about the initiation of his great masterwork. This is what Nietzsche tell us:

> Now I shall relate the history of *Zarathustra*. The fundamental conception of this work, the idea of the eternal recurrence, this highest formula of affirmation that is at all attainable, belongs in August 1881: it was penned on a sheet with the notation underneath, "6000 feet beyond man and time" ... It was on these two walks that the whole of *Zarathustra I* occurred to me, and especially Zarathustra himself as a type: rather, he *overtook me* ...[29]

> ... Has anyone at the end of the nineteenth century a clear idea of what poets of strong ages have called *inspiration*? If not, I will describe it. – If one had the slightest residue of superstition left in one's system, one could hardly reject altogether the idea that one is merely incarnation, merely mouthpiece, merely a medium of overpowering forces. The concept of revelation – in the sense that suddenly, with indescribable certainty and subtlety, something becomes *visible*, audible, something that shakes one to the last depths and throws one down – that merely describes the facts. One hears,

one does not seek; one accepts, one does not ask who gives; like lightning, a thought flashes up, with necessity, without hesitation regarding its form – I never had any choice.

A rapture whose tremendous tension occasionally discharges itself in a flood of tears – now the pace quickens involuntarily, now it becomes slow; one is altogether beside oneself, with the distinct consciousness of subtle shudders and of one's skin creeping down to one's toes; a depth of happiness in which even what is most painful and gloomy does not seem something opposite but rather conditioned, provoked, a *necessary* color in such a superabundance of light; an instinct for rhythmic relationships that arches over wide spaces of forms ...

... Everything happens involuntarily in the highest degree but as in a gale of a feeling of freedom, of absoluteness, of power, of divinity. – The involuntariness of image and metaphor is strangest of all; one no longer has any notion of what is an image or a metaphor: everything offers itself as the nearest, most obvious, simplest expression ... This is *my* experience of inspiration; I do not doubt that one has to go back thousands of years in order to find anyone who could say to me, "it is mine as well."[30]

KS: It's a remarkable passage.

WG: It is indeed. Reflecting on this passage, it is small wonder that Jung later wrote of Goethe, his greatest cultural and spiritual exemplar, and of his masterwork, *Faust*, in the same terms that he wrote of Nietzsche and *Zarathustra*: as vehicles or vessels of numinous revelation.[31] Otto's notion of numinosity is implied by the overwhelming power of such creative inspiration: the finite human is pervaded by his experience of the Holy in such a way that this individual is unconditionally and simultaneously attracted, repulsed, and awed by the experience itself. There is nothing that distinguishes this all-encompassing experience from its object, the Absolute, and the subject who undergoes such an experience is subsumed and even negated by the experiential quality of the encounter. For Nietzsche, numinous experience is not so much to be interpreted as the encounter with the Holy as it is to be understood as the lived recognition of the primal Will to Power. In experiential terms, the principle of the immediate awareness of fundamental self-transformation is the same in both cases.

Several of the self-transforming experiences of Zarathustra, Nietzsche's greatest literary creation, are truly numinous in nature. Zarathustra has an interesting mythological background which Jung details at the beginning of his published seminar on this book. Nietzsche seemed to be looking to the East for inspiration here. He was looking to the ancient Persian tradition, in particular. The Iranian prophet Zoroaster, upon whom Zarathustra is modeled, preached about the eternal conflict between Ahura Mazda, the good god of wisdom and light, and Ahriman, the god of darkness and falsehood (and the prototype of the Old Testament Satan). The cosmic drama would be consummated with the victory of Ahura Mazda and his adherents over Ahriman and his followers. But in his masterwork Nietzsche's Zarathustra is the prophet not of Ahura Mazda, a transcendent cosmic deity of ethical goodness, but rather of the *Übermensch*, the Superman or Overman.

The Superman or Overman is not a personal individual as ordinarily understood, but an individual constituting a new humanity as a whole. This is Nietzsche's new myth of the meaning of "the whole," a non-transcendent yet trans-personal "whole" which is culturally transformative. This "new humanity" will, in effect, have to assume the functions of the now deceased God of Christian Platonism. The new humanity will be responsible for the origination, preservation, and consummation of a new "universe" or *Weltanschauung*. This is Nietzsche's ultimate vision.

KS: Zarathustra, along with Nietzsche himself, is the prophet of this new humanity, then.

WG: Yes. In *Zarathustra*, the prophet merges or fuses with what is prophesied, the Overman. There are other important mythical elements involved here. The Overman merges into Dionysus, the divine-demonic figure in Nietzsche's first book, *The Birth of Tragedy* (*Die Geburt der Tragödie*). And Dionysus merges with Ariadne, the former consort of Theseus, to constitute what Nietzsche calls "complementary man," masculine and feminine, united in a new union, what Jung later is to call the *hieros gamos* or sacred marriage.[32] Marriage, like Nietzsche's Overman, expresses complementarity and the coincidence of opposites.

KS: The principle of complementarity that is fundamental here, I would say, echoes Hegel's emphasis upon a synthetic unity of opposites in the attainment of integrated wholeness. I think also of the Taoist union of the principles of *yin* and *yang*.

WG: Yes, and I'd like to talk about Taoism a bit later, in relation to Jung. This all brings us back to Otto's notion of numinosity as a union of the rational and irrational elements of true religious experience. Complementary man, representing the multi-dimensional self as a creative organization of mainly unconscious drives and instincts, merges into the "higher man" and the "higher man" into the authentic "philosopher" and "free spirit." The free spirit must recognize himself as a complex of drives and instincts, both rational and irrational, both Apollonian and Dionysian. This is Nietzsche's definition of the truly self-realized individual.

KS: I know that you founded a small reading group here at Bowdoin which has studied Jung's published seminar on Nietzsche's *Zarathustra* carefully, line by line, for more than a decade.

WG: It's the only way to appreciate such a complicated and inspirational work, as Jung showed us with his seminar that lasted from 1934 to 1939. *Zarathustra* itself is saturated with Biblical and classical imagery and with the aura of archetypal energy. Having read it over a period of years, it is difficult now to imagine a more exciting book. I remember Tillich saying in a lecture that when he was a chaplain in the German army in World War I, it seemed that practically every other German soldier had a copy of *Zarathustra* in his knapsack. Nietzsche's influence upon European thinking from the late 19th century through the first quarter of the 20th century, and in many ways even up until the present, was enormous.

KS: Let me try to summarize a bit. Nietzsche was the first philosopher who had diagnosed the cultural disease of his time as that of nihilism and who had advocated the ideal of the Superman or *Übermensch* as a remedy. From a cultural point of view, it would seem that Nietzsche was responding to the dangers of a typically bourgeois culture whose "herd mentality" or excessive conformism was making its members unfit for the psychological and spiritual challenges of a changing world. By focusing on the development of selfhood and the principle of self-realization from a depth-psychological perspective, Nietzsche indicated an inherent capacity for personal self-transcendence that could assist in supplanting the need for those institutions such as the Christian religion which were becoming viewed more and more as dogmatic illusions. The central teaching of the Eternal Recurrence provides redemption or liberation from nihilism through an acceptance of the Will to Power, the will to create by "letting things be and become," as you put it. You have said that the belief in Eternal Recurrence is the absolutization or universalization of the concept of self-realization: Pindar's maxim "Become what you are."

WG: Yes. "Become" implies radical self-transformation and "what you are" designates the "Self," that deep ground and center of the human personality which is largely hidden and unknown and which must be brought to the light and life of consciousness. The Self consists of both rational and irrational elements, both conscious and unconscious, and so self-realization must integrate both aspects of the human psyche.

KS: One of my favorite novels, Hermann Hesse's *Steppenwolf*, describes this process of self-realization as an integration of the rational and the irrational sides of human existence. I know that Hesse had been highly influenced by Nietzsche and had also come into contact with Jung and Jungian thought. Many of his novels concern the idea of self-realization, especially in terms of creative individuality. From Hesse as well as from Nietzsche and Jung, we learn that the path to the deep ground and center of the personality must be forged by each individual in his or her own way, since each individual is a unique pattern of drives and instincts. I know that Nietzsche bases his entire philosophical outlook upon the principle of creative individuality.

WG: That's right. Nietzsche concludes thus in *Zarathustra*: "This is now *my* way. Where is *yours*? *The* way does not exist." And as you point out, Hesse also followed this individuating route to a discovery of the inner Self, rejecting merely collectivist and conventionalist notions of the human personality. The Nietzschean emphasis on multi-dimensional selfhood and each individual's unique pathway to the Self has led me directly to Jung and his concept of individuation. As I indicated previously, Jung was positively indebted to Nietzsche, especially when we equate self-realization with individuation.

KS: So let's concentrate now, given this connection, on Nietzsche's influence upon Jung.

Jung on Nietzsche and Individuation

WG: Right. I'd like to focus here on Jung's three major encounters with *Zarathustra*.

Few people can rival Jung in his knowledge of *Also Sprach Zarathustra*. He read it first as a young medical student at the University of Basel in 1898, found it "morbid," and feared that he, like Nietzsche, might go mad, since he obscurely recognized a profound philosophical and psychological affinity with the famed sage. Jung had heard about Nietzsche as a familiar figure on the streets of Basel, although he never met him. Yet when he read *Zarathustra* he sensed something – a second personality, a kind of "numinous" personality in distinction from the everyday personality of which he heard.

It made him recall something of which he had been aware in his own personal experience from his earliest youth: his "personality No. 2," which sharply contrasted with his ordinary, everyday "personality No.1."[33] Jung characterizes the numinosity of the former personality as the "irruption of the imperishable into the transitory." These "break-ins" or "invasions" into ordinary consciousness were also described vividly in Nietzsche's comments on inspiration in *Ecce Homo*, which I read to you. These invasions occurred primarily through dreams, visions, and extraordinary coincidences. Because of his life-long direct experience of a personality No. 2, Jung felt as a young man in his first encounter with Zarathustra that he too might go the way of Nietzsche and become subsumed by the numinous energies within him.

KS: And Jung returned to the text later in life.

WG: Yes. Jung's second encounter with Zarathustra was in the winter of 1914-1915, after World War I began. In 1912, Jung had broken with Freud, even after Freud had designated him as his successor. Jung could not stomach Freud's dogmatically insistent view of the sexual etiology of neuroses, since he felt strongly that manifold psychological malfunctions were much more a matter of a lack of a real sense of meaning or purpose in one's life.[34] In other words, according to Jung and in opposition to Freud, psychological problems are fundamentally spiritual or religious in nature rather than strictly libidinal.

KS: Jung's departure from his mentor must have been liberating to some degree.

WG: Yes, but the break with Freud was also very traumatic for Jung. In 1913, Jung had a very grievous foreboding of World War I, in which he experienced a vision of Europe drenched in blood.[35] From the years 1913 to 1917, he underwent what he calls his famous "Confrontation with the Unconscious," as depicted in Chapter VI of his autobiography, a confrontation that followed his break with Freud. One commentator aptly describes it as Jung's internalization of World War I. It was an extremely severe test of selfhood requiring every bit of stamina that he had.[36] And during this period, it is interesting to know that he read and annotated *Zarathustra* as a kind of prophylaxis. He also avoided complete isolation, and kept up an active social life and professional practice. During this period, the basic ideas of his later analytical psychology originated in the crucible of an intense self-transformation.

Jung's third and last major engagement with *Zarathustra* occurred during the five years preceding the outbreak of World War II in 1939. He conducted a weekly seminar in Zurich with a group of some fifty people. Many of these people, like Marie Louise von Franz, went on to become major disciples, analysts, scholars, and teachers in the Jungian tradition. For many years, transcripts of the seminar were privately circulated and remained unpublished. In 1988, however, the seminar was published by Princeton University Press in two volumes comprising some 1500 pages. It is regarded as the most searching and comprehensive psychological commentary on Nietzsche's masterwork in existence.

KS: Let's talk a bit about Jung's actual theory of the psyche as it developed over the years in relation to his Nietzschean influences.

WG: By that year of 1939, Jung had developed his own system, a theory that was already significantly influenced by Nietzsche. Of fundamental importance, as I remarked at the outset, is his concept of the individuation process as self-realization. Individuation is a process of moving toward a vital equilibrium of two polar energies. One pole, the ego, is inferior to the other in sheer power but superior in actual consciousness. The ego is the rational, morally responsible element of the personality, which Jung describes as a "light in the forest of being."

The other pole Jung calls "the archetype of the Self", or simply "Self" (sometimes uncapitalized). The term "archetype" derives from the Greek, meaning "prime imprinter," and refers in a Jungian sense to universal instinctual patterns in the psyche. The "Self" is infinitely superior to the ego in power but inferior in actual (but not potential) consciousness. The Self is the ground and center of meaning of the Collective Unconscious, which is the objective, trans-personal, autonomous, essentially numinous psyche. Jung's point here is implicit in Nietzsche and is also one which Tillich later takes up as foundational in his theology, as we shall see. Although each thinker deals with the matter in his own unique way – philosophical, psychological, or theological – it is original with none. Within the German-speaking mystical tradition, it goes back at least to Meister Eckhart in the 14th century with his distinction between the Godhead (*Gottheit*) – the ultimate source of all particular ideas or images of God – and God (*Gott*).

KS: Can this "archetype of the Self" be known in a cognitive sense?

WG: The archetype of the Self cannot be known in and of itself, just as Otto's *numinosum*, Tillich's Being-Itself, or Eckhart's Godhead cannot be known in and of themselves. All we know of the archetype of the Self are archetypal images (*Bilder*) that are part of our collective or individual consciousness. Those images are as valid and as real as anything in our experience. Along with our concepts of objective reality (*esse in re*) and conceptual reality (*esse in intellectu*), there is psychological reality (*esse in anima*) as an autonomous affective content, co-equal with the others and serving as an intermediary between them.

It is interesting to note in this connection that in his *Varieties of Religious Experience* of 1902, William James writes among his philosophical conclusions that "*as soon as we deal with private and personal phenomena as such, we deal with realities in the completest sense of the term.*"[37] I would add to the category of "private and personal phenomena" (such as immediate feelings) *archetypal images*, as numinously charged configurations of representations directly present to consciousness.

KS: So what are some examples of these images of the archetype of the Self?

WG: Some of Jung's leading examples of archetypal images of the Self are Nietzsche's Zarathustra and the Superman, Goethe's Faust, the

Buddha, and the Christ. It is important to emphasize that while Jung is firmly rooted in Western cultural traditions and deplores cultural dilettantism, his perspective on the Self is truly global, even *sub specie aeternitatis*. The concept of Self is derived as much from the Indian concept of *atman* as it is from Nietzsche's notion of Overman. *Atman* appears well-suited to express the (otherwise incomprehensible and inexpressible) universal and eternal Brahmanic aspect of the experience of the Self in the ego's transformative and existential engagement with it.

The case is not entirely dissimilar with respect to the Tao, or the Way, that fundamental principle of Chinese philosophy and religion. There's much to be said, actually, about the parallels between Jungian thought and Taoist thought, and I'd like to elaborate on these parallels further on.   Jung's cross-cultural and transcendental psychological perspective has led Cambridge University philosopher of religion, Don Cupitt, to describe Jung, with only some exaggeration, as "the first genuinely multi-faith thinker." [38]

KS: You've often mentioned the importance of Jung's notion of "active imagination." How does that relate to the archetype of the Self and the individuation process?

WG: The method of "active imagination" is the key to the process of individuation, understood as a principle of *becoming* psychologically *whole* in terms of the relation between ego and Self. And while it is a complex process, it may be summed up as a letting oneself (one's ego) be confronted with and engaged by the numinously charged representations which emerge from the autonomous unconscious psyche and taking a creatively rational and personally responsible attitude toward them. Without such an attitude, such a "confrontation with the Unconscious" may lead to nihilistic self-disintegration rather than to self-realization.   A deeply personal encounter with one's unconscious energies is provoked by a state of crisis and psychic instability which is characteristic of nihilism in the profound sense. Within such a condition, one is forced upon a choice: either one may succumb passively to the abyss of nihilism or one may actively discover and realize his or her true Self.

We can see how Nietzsche's philosophy, especially *Thus Spake Zarathustra*, was fruitfully interpreted by Jung as a *spiritual exercise*. Jung views Nietzsche's encounter with Zarathustra out of which his masterwork was born as comparable to his own initiatory experience in which analytical psychology originated. In his insightful discussion of the spiritual dimension of Jung's distinctive psycho-spiritual method of "active imagination," Elie Humbert, a prominent French analyst, calls attention to three German terms which he calls "action words" and which sum up Jung's own conscious activity as a spiritual practice in engaging the deliverances of the unconscious:

(1) The first of these terms is *Geschehenlassen*, "to let happen," which means that Jung did not deny, resist, or attack the emotionally-freighted images which assailed him in his ordeal.

(2) At the same time – and this is crucial – Jung did not allow himself to be swamped and swallowed up by his experience, as opposed to Nietzsche. This is indicated by the second action word, *Betrachten*: to consider, to impregnate, to put oneself at a distance, to contemplate.

(3) The final and most dramatic action term is *Sich auseinandersetzen*, meaning "to confront oneself with," or consciousness's "having it out with" the unknown which infinitely transcends it.

These three terms express the essence of Jung's decisive and Zarathustra-like initiatory experience as the departure point for a spiritual exercise. In Humbert's view, these terms identify the experiential source of his works and creativity. And they help us to understand more clearly the type of creative experience that led Nietzsche to write his masterwork, *Zarathustra*.

An important parallel that points to the essential spiritual foundations of Jung's psychology is seen when we view the work of Meister Eckhart. Jung's embodiment of the spiritual modes of *Geschehenlassen, Betrachten,* and *Sich auseinandersetzen* remarkably parallel three key terms in the experience and thought of the great 14th century mystic and philosopher. *Geschehenlassen* parallels Eckhart's *Gelazenheit* – releasement.[39] *Betrachten* parallels Eckhart's idea of *Abgeschiedenheit* or detachment.[40] *Sich auseinandersetzen* suggests Eckhart's famous *Durchbruch*, breakthrough, to the *Grund* (ground) or *Gottheit* (Godhead), comparable to Jung's discovery of the archetype of the Self (*das Selbst*) as the ultimate center of meaning of the unconscious.[41]

KS: And so these spiritual modes, as articulated by Eckhart and Humbert, help us to understand more clearly the parallels between the initiatory or creative experience of Jung and that of Nietzsche.

WG: Yes. And these modes help us to define the *general* basis on which Jung critiqued Nietzsche. Both Nietzsche and Jung are cited by Ellenberger, in his *The Discovery of the Unconscious*, as prime examples of what he calls "creative illness."[42] Jung as a physician, in particular, follows in the tradition of the "wounded healer" prefigured in the shaman of primal cultures. The "creative" element is really manifold but its essence, shared by Nietzsche and Jung, is the discovery mentioned above that, in addition to objective reality and conceptual reality, there is psychological reality. Nietzsche had forecast that in the future the major avenue of approach to traditional philosophical and theological problems would be through psychology, and Jung is a major pioneering exemplification of the truth of that assertion. For him *anima* or *psyche* is an autonomous imaginal and emotional entity, coequal if not superior in its reality to both mind and matter and an intermediary between them.

KS: So the psychological crises that were experienced by Nietzsche and Jung were creative illnesses in that they led to their great insights into the human condition?

WG: That is my understanding of the situation. Nietzsche's creativity and illness, as with Jung's, were closely intertwined. Nietzsche spent the last decade of his life in a state of utter paralysis and psychosis. Jung's confrontation with the Unconscious appears to have been a perilous flirtation with a similar danger, but he narrowly escaped Nietzsche's fate. Most interesting is how he explains the difference between Nietzsche and himself in terms of his own psychological theory.[43] Jung's theory can be described most briefly as an original synthesis of Freud's psychoanalysis as based on the concept of the ego (the "I") and Nietzsche's concept of the Self as based on the distinction, but not the separation or the merger, between the Self and the ego. What Jung calls the archetype of the Self is both the centerpoint and the circumference of the Collective Unconscious or "objective psyche." It is a dynamic potential for self-realization, an illustration of which, up to a point, is Nietzsche's prophet Zarathustra and the "Beyond man" which he proclaimed.

KS: So Jung criticizes Nietzsche in a sense for having succumbed in a most negative manner to the archetypal and unconscious energies of his psyche.

WG: Yes, generally speaking. The *specific* insight, upon which Jung's critique of Nietzsche was based, occurs in the last stanza of a very brief poem that Nietzsche wrote at Sils Maria sometime between 1882 and 1884, when *Zarathustra* was being composed:

> *Da wurde eins zu zwei*
> *Und Zarathustra ging an mir vorbei.*
> Then ... one became two
> And Zarathustra passed by me.

Jung puts great emphasis on these lines early in his published seminar on Nietzsche's masterwork.[44] Implicit in these lines is the distinction between Nietzsche's ego, the "me" that is passed by, and Zarathustra, experienced as an autonomous, numinous, supra-ordinate personality in his psychological make-up.   Jung, as mentioned previously, had from early childhood similar experiences of what he calls a "personality No. 1," ordinary and everyday, and a "personality No. 2," comprising insistent self-representations or images of numinous power and meaning. Jung was able to come to terms with his No. 2 personality and survive. But Nietzsche did not, Jung argues, because his ego was consumed by the numinous energy of the archetypal images.

KS: Would it be safe to say, then, that Nietzsche's emphases upon creative individuality and the mainly unconscious Will to Power may have been an indirect expression of this inner turmoil involving the ego?

WG: That is likely, which is not to take away at all from Nietzsche's overall philosophical teachings.   On the personal level, Nietzsche succumbed to what Jung calls "ego-inflation" and what others might call "megalomania" or "malignant narcissism."   Nietzsche was primarily an artist, whose raw materials were his many illnesses. In reference to Nietzsche's statement that "I am one thing, my writings are another," Jung responded: "I judge a philosopher by whether he is able to serve as an example." For all his inspired brilliance, Nietzsche failed Jung's test.

KS: How do we relate this personal failure to Nietzsche's view of himself as "the perfect nihilist?"

WG: We might say that Nietzsche recognized and suffered the advent of nihilism – psychologically, spiritually, philosophically – so intensely that he was not able to overcome this existential crisis in the same way that his own paradigm of self-transcendence, Zarathustra, was able to rise to the task of self-creation: the acceptance of his own being in terms of his own becoming. Nietzsche was brilliant enough to diagnose the spiritual problem of his time and to propose a new spirituality which might emerge from a recognition of multi-dimensional selfhood – but he was *personally* too weak in a psychological sense to follow the example of his own writings.

In Jung's view, Nietzsche had a primal experience of an autonomous, numinous personality – Zarathustra – but did not know how to handle it because he lacked the advantages that Jung derived from the cautionary example of Nietzsche's prior experience. Jung had had experiences of personalities No. 1 and No. 2 from early boyhood, while in Nietzsche's case Zarathustra irrupted suddenly into his experience when he was about forty.

KS: So Jung was much more successful in dealing with his own numinous energies and archetypal images.

WG: Jung had developed a psychological method for dealing with such an extraordinary and momentous phenomenon. Nietzsche lacked a stable symbol-system to "schematize" his intensely affect-laden numinous experience.   Overwhelmed, Nietzsche identified with Zarathustra, the Overman, Dionysus, and other archetypal images. Unable consistently and in a stable manner to differentiate his ego from these manifestations of the Self, his ego was consumed by them.

Further, Jung interprets Nietzsche as anticipating his own fate in the symbolic fall of the rope-dancer in Part I of *Zarathustra*. Knocked off the rope from behind by the Buffoon, the rope-dancer fell to his death. According to Jung, Nietzsche identified with the rope-dancer as he had with so many other figures in *Zarathustra*. He exposed himself to the overwhelming powers of the numinous and was unable, like Zarathustra or Job, to rise above the fundamental tension between Being and Non-Being, a tension which defines nihilism in its deepest sense. I refer back to Otto's notion of the numinous as a coincidence of opposites in terms of a tremendous and fascinating mystery, with Job as a perfect illustration of an individual who successfully confronted the challenges of the numinous.

KS: The "creative illness" of Nietzsche certainly seems to echo the intense inner turmoil and doubt that plagued Job.

WG: Yes. It should be pointed out here that Jung, working independently of Otto in his *Answer to Job* (1952) – the only book he wrote of which he said he would not change a word – regards the story of Job as a prime example of the individuation process. This self-realizing process of "becoming whole" consists essentially of making the Unconscious conscious, of bringing the Unconscious to consciousness. The former, the collective Unconscious or "objective psyche," is the undifferentiated, numinously charged energy symbolized by Yahweh, while the latter, limited ego-consciousness, is symbolized by Job. The result of their momentous encounter is the emergence within the whole divine-human complex of a new consciousness of what it means to be human on the part of the divine. Although Jung does not emphasize the reciprocal emergent human consciousness of what it means to be divine, his main point is that Christ is the "answer to Job" as an archetypal image of the Self (*das Selbst, the itself*). Christ, echoing the self-transformed consciousness of Job, represents the vital union or coincidence of the opposites of the finite human and the infinite divine.

KS: These images of the human encounter with the numinous, and the resulting transformation of human consciousness, also seem to point to a type of liberation or sense of freedom.

WG: Exactly. Jungian scholar Edward Edinger agrees with Jung that, more than any other modern writer since Goethe, Nietzsche re-discovered the numinous as the source of creative freedom, and that in the process he became its sacrificial victim because he stepped too far beyond conventional and traditional limits of the human condition. The lessons of Job, Zarathustra, Nietzsche, and Jung lead us, actually, to Tillich's philosophical theology as based on his concept of human nature as *finite freedom* and on his ideal of human life as a fundamental process of self-realization that requires "the courage to be." Such existential courage, epitomized by Job and Zarathustra, should be viewed as especially necessary after having considered the extreme dangers of nihilism and the associated dangers of a personal confrontation with the Unconscious.

Tillich on Self-Realization and Finite Freedom

KS: Tell me more specifically, then, about Tillich and his background and how he fits into the picture.

WG: By middle-age, Paul Tillich had achieved great eminence in Germany as a philosopher and theologian, having taught at a number of major universities. In the process he incurred the displeasure of the Nazis due to his very active involvement in a movement known as "Religious Socialism." When the Nazis assumed power in 1933, he emigrated to America, where his friend Reinhold Niebuhr got him a job at Union Theological Seminary, where he taught for many years. He also taught at Columbia University and lectured widely throughout American colleges and universities and published many influential books. Following his retirement at Union he served a term as University Professor at Harvard and ended his career at the University of Chicago, holding a very distinguished professorship. He died in 1965.

KS: Is there a way for you to distill the essence of Tillich's teaching, in spite of the fact that his writings are so wide-ranging and varied?

WG: Well, I would say that Tillich's main effort was to bring together philosophy of a secular or apparently non-religious kind, especially existentialism, and Christian theology as understood by an individual who had lived through World War I intimately and who was quite conversant with many turbulent currents of modernity.[45]

KS: If you would, please outline Tillich's overall teaching in order to relate his ideas to those of Nietzsche and Jung, especially in confronting the problem of nihilism.

WG: When teaching about the core of Tillich's philosophical theology, I usually deal first with four basic propositions and then turn to seven basic points regarding his concept of self-realization.

In a series of lectures that he gave at Harvard and elsewhere, Tillich traced the development of modern Western religious thought. He draws his prevailing theme from Nicholas of Cusa – late Renaissance cardinal, mathematician, and mystic. The theme is that of the *coincidentia oppositorum*, the coincidence of opposites, which I have been emphasizing here. His own best example of that theme is his concept of basic human nature as essentially *finite freedom*. Humanity possesses a unique and quasi-divine creative freedom, but at the same time is closely and ineluctably limited by certain circumstances.[46] I'll spell out this idea in more detail as I turn more specifically to Tillich's notion of self-realization.

The second proposition concerns Tillich's definition of the essence of religion, as that which concerns us unconditionally (*"was uns unbedingt angeht"*).[47] This is what Tillich means by another, much more familiar term he uses for the same idea: "ultimate concern." Genuine religion and ultimate concern are synonyms for him. Ultimate concern transcends that which concerns us provisionally or on a transient, fleeting, contingent, finite basis.

Tillich draws the third proposition from traditional wisdom, from the kind of existentialism that is represented in Nietzsche's thought, and from the kind of depth-psychology that is represented by Freud and especially by Jung (whom Tillich favored, I think, as against Freud). It concerns the human condition, which Tillich describes as one of "tragic and universal self-estrangement." This returns us, of course, to the fundamental spiritual problem of our time, nihilism, in which self-estrangement or self-alienation is a central manifestation of a confrontation with Non-Being or Nothingness.[48]

The fourth proposition is distinctive of Tillich as a self-described theologian of culture. For him religion and culture are related like two sides of one coin, religion being the substance, and culture the form.[49] A culture is the self-expression of its ultimate concern, its true religion. Self-realization, then, should be understood as both an individual and collective process, just as we should define nihilism as an individual and cultural phenomenon.

KS: Tillich, then, also has a concept of self-realization.

WG: Most definitely. Like Nietzsche and Jung, he begins with Pindar's "Become what you are," and then after an ellipsis adds "created to create." For Tillich self-realization is dialectical, following the Hegelian method of reasoning to some degree. Self-realization is a dynamic interaction between creative freedom as limited by createdness and finitude as transcended by creative freedom. Creativity is the essential expression of human freedom and createdness is the essential expression of human finitude. Thus, the essence of being human as finite freedom is a coincidence of opposites, the paradoxical presence of infinite, creative freedom amidst the finitude of human existence.

Although Tillich's interpretation of self-realization obviously differs from Nietzsche's Will to Power and Eternal Recurrence and Jung's process of individuation, and in addition is explicitly Christian, it nevertheless presupposes their work and overlaps with them in addressing the fundamental philosophical, psychological, and theological problem of nihilism.   Tillich uses the existentialist philosophy represented by Nietzsche (and developed by Martin Heidegger) and the depth-psychology represented by Jung as essential to a better understanding of humanity's tragic and universal self-estrangement.   Fundamentally, human beings – individually and collectively -- are profoundly self-divided, as the Greek tragedians, St. Augustine, and many others had taught. For Tillich, the ground of this self-division is primal anxiety or *Ur-Angst*, which is the apprehension of universal Non-Being, of *das Nichts* or the *nihil*, of Nothingness. He defines the apprehension of Non-Being as "awareness of that element of non-being (of the negation of what one is) which is identical with finitude, the coming from nothing and the going toward nothing." [50]

KS: The fact that this confrontation with Non-Being and with one's own finitude often leads to anxiety or *Angst* is a point that is clearly made by Kierkegaard and by Heidegger.

WG: Yes. And Tillich distinguishes sharply between primal and neurotic anxiety. The latter can be addressed by psychotherapy, by medication, or by some combination of the two. One can alleviate or even eliminate neurotic anxiety, but primal anxiety is inexpungible as a necessary condition of existence in finite freedom. Tillich's analysis of nihilism, based on the notion of primal anxiety, and its resolution in the form of self-realization may be summarized and concluded in the following seven points.

Primal anxiety as a universal and necessary condition of human existence manifests itself to human awareness in three major pairs of experiential realities: "Finitude and death, guilt and condemnation, emptiness and meaninglessness."

Primal anxiety can never be eliminated, but it can be overcome by what Tillich calls "the courage to be ... in spite of" (*"Der Mut zum Sein ...trotz"*).[51]

As primal anxiety is a manifestation to human awareness of Non-Being, so *courage to be in spite of* is the manifestation of the meaning and power of Being-Itself.[52]

Being-Itself is Tillich's term for Godhead or Deity, like the *Gottheit* of Meister Eckhart previously mentioned, and therefore not unlike Otto's numinous and Jung's Self. It is the unconditioned ground of all particular representations of the Divine to human consciousness and the true object of ultimate concern.[53]

The *courage to be in spite of* as the manifestation to human awareness of the meaning and power of Being-Itself emerges in near-tragic, Job-like circumstances. A new form of spirituality appears in an original first-hand experience after a second-hand or personally inauthentic (merely ego- or collective-generated) idea of God has disappeared in some form of primal anxiety. This phenomenon is aptly illustrated in Job's response to Jahweh after the latter's speech to Job from the whirlwind: "I had heard of thee by the hearing of the ear,/ But now my eye sees thee; / Therefore I despise myself,/ And repent in dust and ashes." (Job 42:4-6) The Job-like experience exemplifies *the courage to be* which, says Tillich, is *"rooted in the God who appears when God has disappeared in the anxiety of doubt."*[54] Quite unlike Nietzsche but in a way similar to Jung, Tillich regards the Christ, as Jung put it in his famous book of that title, as *The Answer to Job.* Tillich defines the essence of the Christian message as "the New Being in Jesus as the Christ conquering existence under the conditions of existence."[55] These conditions imply the Non-Being of "finitude and death, guilt and condemnation, emptiness and meaninglessness."

"The courage to be" is one of Tillich's synonyms for faith, the central and basic concept of his theology. "Ultimate concern" is, however, the foremost synonym for faith in his masterwork, *Systematic Theology*, where it is described as an abstraction from Jesus' two great commandments, the unlimited love of God and love of one's neighbor as oneself. Faith transcends all particular and preliminary concerns through its ultimate participation of "the whole being in unambiguous or eternal life." It is an immediate awareness or "feeling of having a necessary, unique and incomparable place in the whole of being."[56]

Finally, considering the prominence of creative illness in the life and work of Nietzsche and Jung, it seems appropriate to emphasize Tillich's concept of "religious health."[57] It illustrates what he has identified as the basic theme of the coincidence of opposites (*coincidentia oppositorum*) and it encapsulates his abiding interest in philosophy, theology, and psychology. He uses the German term

"*Heil*," which denotes wholeness and eternal salvation as well as health in a comprehensive sense. Tillich expresses this unity of important and diverse human concerns as follows: "Religious health is the state of being grasped by the Spirit, enabling us to transcend our religion and return to it in the same experience."[58] In other words, religious health is the condition in which we are paradoxically subsumed, liberated, and affirmed by the presence of that which concerns us ultimately, the ground of our being and the source of genuine meaning in our lives.

KS: Again, let me try to summarize a bit at this point from what I have learned. We have covered a good amount of territory thus far. Tillich addresses the problem of nihilism or the confrontation with Non-Being, which provokes a reciprocal recognition of Being-Itself. Tillich's proposal for a cure is an existential-spiritual "courage to be in spite of." This is an attitude which forces us to recognize the true ground of our being and selfhood and to overcome primal anxiety in the face of Nothingness (usually in the form of death or the sheer contingency of human life). A new form of spirituality, bridging secular existentialism and Christian theology, is required in the face of the decline of institutional Christianity. The emergence of this new spirituality is occasioned, as Tillich shows us, by the individual's confrontation with Non-Being, just as Nietzsche and Jung were driven to highly original insights into the spiritedness of self-realization through their confrontations with the psychological reality of the Unconscious.

WG: Right. It is the confrontation with Non-Being that is crucial here in our attempts to address and to overcome the problem of nihilism. And these considerations over the years have led me to consider the distinctive contributions of Karlfried Graf Dürckheim and his emphasis upon "the shock of Non-Being." These considerations can assist us in elaborating upon the extensive and profound character of the new spirituality that has been emerging, in my opinion.

KS: Let's turn to Dürckheim, then, Bill. Again, please provide me with some background on this important but obscure thinker. I have heard little about him. But I can already begin to see how he fits into the overall scheme of things that you have started to lay out.

Dürckheim's "Shock of Non-Being"

WG: Karlfried Graf Dürckheim, who died in 1988 at the age of ninety-six, was born of Bavarian Catholic nobility. As a young man he served for forty-six months as an officer in the German army in WW I on all fronts. After the war, he earned doctorates in both philosophy and psychology at the Universities of Kiel and Munich, respectively. He also taught at Kiel and Leipzig.

KS: How did this young soldier with a Bavarian Catholic background become a Zen master in the course of his life?

WG: Dürckheim seems to have had a profound curiosity about various world religions. We know that, in the course of later travels, he arrived in Japan in 1937, where he studied Zen Buddhism under several masters, the best known of whom in the West was D. T. Suzuki. Returning home ten years later, he established what became a world-famous retreat in the Black Forest, which he called the "Center for Existential Formation and Encounter." There he combined experiential, transformational, and methodological elements in a new form of spirituality comprising a dynamic synthesis of historic Christian teaching , Western psychology, and Eastern philosophy.

Although he published many books during his lifetime and was well-known in Europe, he is just beginning to become more widely known in this country. The best and most recent introduction to his thought is entitled *Dürckheim: Dialogue on the Path of Initiation.* His dialogue partner is a French former Roman Catholic priest, Alphonse Goettmann, who converted to Eastern Orthodoxy and who, with his wife Rebecca, established a center of research and meditation called "Bethanie" in eastern France. The Goettmanns are perhaps his greatest living disciples, while Thomas J. Nottingham is the leading proponent and expositor of his views in this country.

One of the key words in the title of the above-mentioned book provides insight into the core of Dürckheim's thinking. "Dialogue" means that he is a dialectical thinker, much like Socrates and Plato and Hegel and Tillich. He emphasizes the interaction of dialogue partners, an interaction which emerges from and at the same time gives rise to a new awareness of an undifferentiated yet mysteriously creative numinous energy, which he calls "Essential Being." "Essential Being" is the central and fundamental term in Dürckheim's thinking. It is similar to Nietzsche's Will to Power, to Jung's Collective Unconscious or objective psyche, and to Tillich's Being-Itself. It is the primordial, undifferentiated, indivisible, creative energy – in the traditional language of religious and mystical thinkers like Meister Eckhart, the Godhead.

KS: You've mentioned earlier how some of the deeply personal experiences of Nietzsche, Jung, and Tillich led to their unique insights and teachings. You mentioned the notion of a "creative illness," for example. Does the same hold true for Dürckheim?

WG: Yes, most definitely. In his autobiographical introduction to this book, Dürckheim tells how he was awakened to Essential Being through experiencing the "shock of Non-Being." This shock was precipitated by the sight of the corpse of a French soldier during his war service.

KS: I think here of the story of Siddhartha Gautama, the young prince who had lived a very sheltered life at the direction of his father. Upon leaving the palace gates at long last as a young man, Siddhartha experienced a similar shock upon seeing a sick person, an elderly person, and then a corpse.

WG: That's a very appropriate parallel to draw here. Gautama, of course, would go on to achieve full meditative and contemplative enlightenment, thereby becoming the Buddha and the founder of Buddhism.

KS: What does it mean, then, to say that one has experienced "the shock of Non-Being?"

WG: The fuller meaning of Dürckheim's first shock of Non-Being was disclosed later when, in the company of his wife, he happened to read the eleventh verse of the *Tao Te Ching*. The verse goes as follows:

> Thirty spokes converge upon a single hub;
> It is on the hole in the center that the use of the cart hinges.
> We make a vessel from a lump of clay;
> It is the empty space within the vessel that makes it useful.

> We make the doors and windows for a room;
> But it is these empty spaces that make the room livable.
> Thus, while the tangible has advantages,
> It is the intangible that makes it useful.[59]

Dürckheim comments on his experience of reading this verse for the first time. He tells us:

> And suddenly it happened! Lightning went through me. The veil was torn asunder, I was awake! I had just experienced "It." Everything existed and nothing existed. Another reality had broken through this world. I myself existed and did not exist. I was seized, enchanted, someplace else and yet here, happy and deprived of feeling, far away and at the same time deeply rooted in things. The reality that surrounded me was suddenly shaped by two poles: one that was the immediately visible, and the other an invisible which was the essence of that which I was seeing. I truly saw Being.[60]

KS: It sounds to me like the type of experience that some, like James Joyce, refer to as an "epiphany."

WG: Yes, it was a true epiphany. This remarkable passage indicates that Dürckheim underwent the Zen experience of *satori*, or ultimate enlightenment, fifteen years before he went to Japan for his decade of Zen training. It is similar to Nietzsche's account of the inspiration of *Zarathustra* and thus to Otto's explanation of the experience of numinosity as a tremendous and fascinating mystery. The experience as described above also parallels Jung's discovery of the Self as "the irruption of the imperishable into the transitory," as well as Tillich's "New Being conquering existence under the conditions of existence."

Dürckheim refers to this as the experience of "Being in that which is" (*"Das Sein in Seienden"*).[61] He regards Meister Eckhart in the fourteenth century, with his idea of the Godhead (*Gottheit*) as the source of all god-ideas, as the greatest master in the West of the conceptualization in experiential and transformational terms of "Being in that which is."[62] The greatest contemporary master, according to Dürckheim, was Zen master D. T. Suzuki.[63]

KS: You had earlier described Jung as a cross-cultural thinker whose teachings, for instance, might be paralleled with those of Taoism. It seems that Dürckheim is also very much a point of intellectual and spiritual intersection between East and West.

WG: Indeed he is. In fact, I have an anecdote that is relevant here. Dürckheim once asked Suzuki to discourse on Asian wisdom. Suzuki began: "Western knowledge looks outside, Eastern knowledge looks within ... But if you look within the way you look without, you make of the within a without."[64] To Dürckheim this was another shock of Non-Being, an insight into the reduction of essential subjectivity or selfhood to a false objectivity that expresses, if not causes, the universal condition of self-forgetting and self-division.

You might also think here of the Jewish existential-mystical thinker, Martin Buber, and his radical distinction between the attitudes of I-Thou and I-It as formulated in his classic text *I and Thou (Ich und Du)*. Buber points out, as Suzuki had obviously done for Dürckheim, that the attitude which views everything around us as mere things or objects also forces us to view *ourselves* as mere things or objects – i.e., looking "within the way you look without." I would say that this over-emphasis on thinghood and objectivity and externality might be understood as a leading manifestation of the nihilistic self-estrangement that Tillich emphasized. Objectification, then, occasions the de-humanization of the individual.

KS: You mentioned that Dürckheim, like Martin Heidegger, emphasizes his recognition of "Being" in the encounter with Non-Being. Could you say more about that?

WG: Dürckheim formulated the experience of Essential Being, an experience arising with the shock of Non-Being, as "transparence to transcendence." "Transparence" should be understood here as clarity of perception and knowledge, as an absence of distortion or confusion in the ways in which we come to grasp ourselves and our environment. "Transcendence" points to a realm or dimension of reality and knowledge which is not confined merely to sense-impressions and external objects, but which should not be taken as "supernatural" or "other-worldly."[65] One thinks of William Blake's famous statement: "If the doors of perception were cleansed, every thing would appear to man as it is – infinite." Following Suzuki, Dürckheim describes entering the path of initiation as learning "to look without the way you ought to look within." Or, as Kierkegaard said, "Truth is subjectivity." Nietzsche also emphasizes the personal, subjective, and perspectival nature of true knowledge, especially of genuine *self*-knowledge.

KS: So, in other words, we must learn to experience and understand the true nature of reality, the reality of the world and of ourselves, in *subjective* terms, in terms of the depths of our Self and Being rather than in terms of value-neutral objects and surface phenomena. This seems to be what you referred to earlier as "psychological reality."

WG: Yes. And in considering self-realization as transparence to transcendence, as awareness of Essential Being, Dürckheim is concerned to do two things: (1) preserve the millennial continuity of the mystical, traditional, and perennial philosophy as it is represented in his synthesis of Christianity and Zen Buddhism; (2) proclaim a new age of the spirit, of self-realization as discovery of the Godhead within.

KS: Would Dürckheim agree with Jung's talk of an "archetype of the Self?" Is there a universal pattern of human selfhood that anchors his notion of self-realization?

WG: Well, let us consider Dürckheim's concept of "Self." He identifies three kinds of selves: (1) the "little self," (2) the "existential self," and (3) the "essential Self." I'll say a bit about each mode of selfhood:
The "little self" is similar to Nietzsche's "last man," to Jung's ego as the constructed personality of the "first half of life," and to Tillich's anguished, self-estranged individual. The "little self" is preoccupied, says Dürckheim, with seeking power, security, prestige, and cumulative knowledge.
The "existential self" is the "authentic self" of humanistic existential philosophers of the twentieth century like Jean-Paul Sartre. Such self-constructed personalities lack awareness of Essential Being realizing itself through them.
Finally, the "essential Self" is an incarnation of Essential Being, the discovery that one's core is the "God within," akin to Paul's "It is no longer I who live, but Christ who lives in me."[66] For Dürckheim the essential Self is in an ethical reality in a crucial sense. It makes itself known primarily through what he calls "the still, small voice."[67] This is the basis for the core Self's mediating decision between the claims of the little and the existential selves.[68]

KS: What consequences for my everyday life does this recognition of an "essential Self" entail?

WG: For Dürckheim personally, the essential Self mandated two difficult sacrificial choices: (1) resignation of a post-World War military vocation and commission; (2) relinquishing proprietorship of his inherited estates.[69] He sacrificed both in order to become a retreat master. Such radical obedience to the subtle, insistent voice of conscience represents the essential Self's initiation upon the innate way, the truth and life of Essential Being.

KS: So Dürckheim's version of self-realization leads obviously to self-affirmation rather than self-denial.

WG: Self-realization is anything but self-denial. Rather it is denial of ego-centrality, emptying of ego-centrality, and sacrifice of ego-centrality. This central contention of Dürckheim is illustrated in the spiritual discipline of breathing.[70] To exhale is to undergo an internal *kenosis*, a death-like self-emptying, while to inhale is to be inspired – literally, breathed into, revitalized, resurrected. We might think here of the Greek root of the word for spirit, "*pneuma*," originally signifying breath, and also of the Latin root of this notion, "*anima*," also originally meaning breath. Breathing is deeply symbolic of what Dürckheim calls "the wheel of metamorphosis" of Essential Being.[71] The archetypal expression of this transformational cycle is the "mutual in-dwelling" of the persons of the Trinity as well as the fiery dynamics of the divine lover, the beloved, and their love in its absolute individuality and indivisibility.[72]

Most striking for me is Dürckheim's interpersonal, ethical application of this idea of "mutual in-dwelling." We have already seen that the essential Self, in response to the still small voice of an awakened conscience, decides between the claims of the little self and the existential self. Yet what about Gospel injunctions to love one's neighbor as oneself, and, toughest of all, to love one's enemies? From the self-transformational perspective of Essential Being and the essential Self, the essential Good is primarily the creation of a numinous inner necessity, and not something merely traditional, conventional, collective, or taken in from the outside. The Gospel ethic, like that of the infinitely compassionate *boddhisattva*, rests upon what Dürckheim calls "acceptance," in particular "accepting the unacceptable."[73]

KS: I suppose that there is a certain danger in espousing an ethic of complete acceptance, isn't there? It could be taken as a sign of passivity and quietism.

WG: Acceptance is not "resignation" but a registering awareness of what is. The concept of acceptance, which really means disinterested love, is prefigured in Nietzsche's Eternal Recurrence and "letting things be and become," in Jung's shadow-recognition and shadow-integration, and in Tillich's "courage to be" as expressed in his famous sermons "You are Accepted" and "Waiting."[74] In a sense, these notions of acceptance and self-acceptance relate back to the ancient Stoic ideal of *amor fati*, a love of one's destiny or fate. To love one's neighbor as oneself is not a new law impossible to obey, nor is it to love one's neighbor as one's little or existential self – which might be disastrous – but rather to discern in the other person one's own essential Self, the Christ, the Godhead within.

KS: Is this a universal ethic? Should it be accepted by everyone? Can it be practiced by anyone?

WG: Well, Dürckheim is not elitist, but he recognizes that the path of initiation is not for everyone. On the other hand, as he puts it, "When the student is ready, the master appears."[75] The case of Alphonse Goettmann is instructive in this respect. He writes that, through contact with Dürckheim and his teaching, "I became conscious of the fact that I was desperately searching outside of myself for that which I carried deep within" – the meaning of Jesus' words "Come, follow me."[76] This was Goettmann's transformational Damascus Road experience, his moment of self-realization.

Dürckheim sagely observes that an experience of awakening is not the same thing as an awakened person.[77] Therefore, in addition to the experiential element in spiritedness, he emphasizes equally the systematically transformational method of asceticism or spiritual practice, following Aquinas in defining it as "a well-ordered work whose result is a constitution of man that expresses the fullness of Being."[78] Zen asceticism is conspicuous in Dürckheim's strong emphasis upon *zazen*, silent sitting and breathing.

KS: For one who is, let us say, a Christian rather than a Zen Buddhist, are there other types of spiritual practice which might lead to the same type of enlightenment and self-realization?

WG: As a matter of fact, Dürckheim also speaks of the "profound efficacy" of the Jesus Prayer as "the Christian mantra par excellence," and regards it as "the closest thing to Zen meditation in the Christian tradition."[79] This prayer, also known as "the prayer of the mind, heart, or spirit," originated in the monasteries of Egypt, Syria, and Mount Athos in the fourth through the seventh centuries. It involves the systematic and eventually self-acting repetition of some version of the words "Lord Jesus Christ, Son of God, have mercy on me, a sinner," along with sitting and breathing exercises. Although Dürckheim praised it highly, it was left to the Goettmanns to write a recently-published book on the subject. The point, however, even for Dürckheim, is not this or that method but the transformational *experience* of "Being in that which is."

KS: Let me attempt to re-cap again, Bill. The key insight lies, it seems, in the numinous experience of "Essential Being" as occasioned by the "shock of Non-Being." This experience is, as you have shown, akin to Nietzsche's inspirational encounter with his inner Zarathustra-personality as a way of overcoming nihilism. It is akin to Jung's confrontation with the Unconscious and recognition of the Self as a deep reservoir of the human personality. It is also related to Tillich's "courage to be" as an acknowledgment of Essential Being in the face of Nothingness. This experiential numinosity could be regarded as a type of "epiphany" or "personal awakening" which follows a recognition of Non-Being and a sudden awareness of the psychological and spiritual dangers of nihilism. Such an experience can only be grasped as a coincidence of opposites, where the opposites might be understood in various ways: as human-divine, finite-infinite, repulsion-fascination, Being-Nothingness, consciousness-Unconscious, and so forth. Only by seeking integrated wholeness, then, can we come to know ourselves more authentically and, in the process, overcome the specters of nihilism and Non-Being.

WG: Without the pursuit of personal wholeness, we might generalize, everything about an individual's existence turns gradually to nihilistic fragmentation and despair.

KS: We've covered quite a bit of ground already on our path from the essence of spiritedness and the spiritual problem of our time to the emergence of a new spirituality. If you would, Bill, help me to summarize our overall results so far in your own words.

WG: Well, to review briefly, *the* question asked and *lived* by Nietzsche, Jung, Tillich, and Dürckheim is the fundamental question of Being and Non-Being, illustrated by Hamlet's famous question: "To be or not to be…". Each of these spiritual philosophers came up with a fundamental notion of self-realization, or self-being, in response to the shock of Non-Being.

I have suggested that the common ground of their thought ultimately echoes Hegel and his basic concept that "The truth is the whole." In his greatest work, *The Phenomenology of Spirit*, Hegel defines *Geist* – Mind or Spirit – as "pure self-recognition in absolute otherness." He also says that Spirit "finds its truth in absolute dismemberment." The abstract truth of Spirit is the dialectical, seemingly paradoxical unity of the opposites of Being and Non-Being, as we find explicitly at the very beginning of the Hegelian Logic, in terms of its initial dialectical lesson. It would seem that Nietzsche, Jung, Tillich, and Dürckheim have, in effect, re-cast Hegel's insight in the form of the dynamic tension between self-realization and nihilism.

But these four thinkers are not merely re-phrasing and updating Hegel. They are engaged in their own fundamental trans-valuational process in thinking about and living out what Tillich calls "ultimate concern." Their basic contention is that our traditional, conventional, collective ideas of God, of Essential Being, of ultimate reality and value, are one-sidedly external and objective, seen as coming to us from the outside. As such they are an evasion of or defense against the necessary realization of the "God within."

KS: Please elaborate on this notion of the "God within."

WG: The God or Godhead within is experienced transformationally as a subtle, supra-ordinate, indivisible power moving in on our egos and thereby pervading our world-percepts and world-constructs, demanding recognition as our true reality. It is Essential Being realized by the essential Self in the shock of Non-Being, to use a blend of Tillich's and Dürckheim's terminology. The obstacle to self-realization is not our egos as such, whose ultimate destiny is taken by many religious believers to be an unambiguous living union with God. The obstacle is ego*tism*. The real nihilism, the real Non-Being, the real Nothingness, is our inveterate, seemingly inexpungible ego-*centeredness*, as manifested in both individual and collective terms.

It is evident in the case of Nietzsche, and scarcely less so in the cases of Jung and Tillich and Dürckheim, that self-realization is not some exercise in self-generated self-esteem. It is a high-risk enterprise; it is life lived near the edge. "Live dangerously!" wrote Nietzsche in one of his most famous aphorisms. He went to the edge, again and again and again. One of his most penetrating – and prophetic – aphorisms was: "And when you look long into the abyss, the abyss also looks into you."[80] Nietzsche wrote this just after he had finished *Zarathustra* in 1886. Tempting the fate he foresaw, Nietzsche fell into the nihilistic abyss that he both dreaded and was drawn to. Jung escaped Nietzsche's fate for reasons that we have already considered.

Tillich's case is somewhat different despite his horrendous experiences in World War I. In his autobiographical sketch, he describes his life as "On the Boundary" between various pairs of opposites. The most significant pair for him as a philosophical theologian was the opposition between philosophy and theology and the oppositions or tensions within philosophy and within theology. His mediational philosophical theology was a creative resolution of these oppositional tensions.

KS: Bill, would you regard these thinkers as "humanistic" philosophers?

WG: Nietzsche, Jung, Tillich, and Dürckheim operate within the paradigm of naturalistic humanism. All rejected what Tillich calls "supernaturalism." According to them, the traditional belief in a Deity that is above and beyond nature and humanity needs to be replaced by the concept of a Deity that is the creatively self-transcendent energy within nature and humanity. Otto calls it "the numinous," Nietzsche calls it "the Will to Power," Jung calls it "the Unconscious" or "Self," Tillich calls it "the meaning and power of Being," and Dürckheim calls it "Essential Being" or "Being in that which is."

Because of the powerful numinous element in their thought, each would reject any kind of conformist or merely naturalistic "secular humanism" and would reject the cultural institutions informed by such humanism as masks of nihilism. The emergent spirituality or spiritedness they represent, each in his own unique and powerful way, is a *coincidentia oppositorum*, a coincidence of opposites that is a negation of nihilism and an affirmation of liberation while still alive.

KS: I now have a far greater understanding of the notions of spiritedness and self-realization than I had at the beginning of this conversation, Bill. The spiritedness involved in the quest for self-realization is really the spiritedness of a struggle, isn't it?

WG: It certainly is, as we can see clearly from the personal lives of these remarkable thinkers. I think here of a relevant excerpt from the thirty-second chapter of Genesis that, in its symbolic power, expresses our concern with the struggle against nihilism, with the experience of the numinous, and with the redemptive rewards of individuation and self-realization. Let me read this passage to remind you of what is at stake here in the struggle to realize one's Self:

> And Jacob was left alone; and there wrestled a man with him until the breaking of the day. And when he saw that he prevailed not against him, he touched the hollow of his thigh; and the hollow of Jacob's thigh was out of joint, as he wrestled with him.
> And he said, "Let me go, for the day breaketh."
> And he said, "I will not let thee go, except thou bless me."
> And he said unto him, "What *is* thy name?" And he said, "Jacob."
> And he said, "Thy name shall be called no more Jacob, but Israel: for as a prince hast thou power with God and with men, and has prevailed."
> And Jacob asked *him*, and said, "Tell *me*, I pray thee, thy name."
> And he said, "Wherefore *is* it *that* thou dost ask after my name?"
> And he blessed him there. (Genesis 32:24-29)

KS: This is a story of the struggle for "the God within?"

WG: It is indeed. A struggle for the God within and a struggle for the attainment of integrated wholeness in a very personal and spiritual sense. These are ultimately the same struggle.

My general point of departure was Hegel's statement that "The truth is the whole." I now wish to highlight another statement by Hegel that throws additional light upon the matter at hand: "The consummation of the infinite End, therefore, consists merely in removing the illusion which makes it seem yet unaccomplished."[81] The spiritedness that characterizes Hegel's bold affirmation of self-realization is shared, as we have seen, in their different ways by Nietzsche, Jung, Tillich, and Dürckheim. Each raises the real possibility of genuine self-realization, of the transcendence of ego-centeredness as a *question* to be *lived*, recalling Rilke's poetic motto with which we began.

KS: We have begun, then, to arrive at an overall philosophical and spiritual teaching based on the foregoing insights and inquiries. Your teaching concerns, most fundamentally, the nature of human spiritedness as a drive for self-realization. Spiritedness involves a coincidence of opposites, including a sometimes ambiguous blending of the rational and the irrational and of both finite and infinite concerns. Spiritedness is your term for that human energy or "courage to be" which aims not merely at psychological harmony, it would seem, but at *the goal of expressing oneself in terms of the Whole.* That is, spiritedness appears to be the human capacity to recognize and to express a holistic connection between one's individual existence and the comprehensive trans-personal unity that conditions this existence. The awareness and exercise of such a connection leads, if I may put it like this, to an "ethic" of *self-conscious self-transcendence.* By actualizing such spiritedness, the self-transcending individual is able to confront and eventually to overcome the nihilistic belief that nothing is essential, that Life possesses no inherent meaning and rests upon no permanent foundations, and that "Truth" is a mere illusion.

WG: Above all, I would like to put emphasis, first and foremost, on *an amplified awareness of the importance of the present moment* in the attainment of wholeness. In doing so, I believe that I am following a long and ancient pathway that stretches back to the Stoic and Epicurean schools of antiquity. This emphasis leads to an acausal, holistic, and synchronistic viewpoint. The thinkers who have most intrigued me over the years present a similar teaching about the ineluctable power of the Present, whether this be realized through Jungian individuation or Nietzschean self-overcoming or Dürckheim's "shock of Non-Being" or Tillich's "ultimate concern."

These thoughts have converged after years of reading and re-reading, line by careful line, selected spiritual classics such as Augustine's *Confessions* and Nietzsche's *Thus Spake Zarathustra* and Jung's *Memories, Dreams, Reflections.* Over the last few years, I have made a careful study of one special book that reflects many of my own beliefs about the nature of philosophy. This book is Pierre Hadot's *Philosophy As a Way of Life: Spiritual Exercises from Socrates to Foucault.*

You see, Hadot views *genuine philosophy as a method of spiritual training and self-responsibility,* a view with which I am much in sympathy.[82] Connected to this definition of philosophy is Hadot's primary emphasis *upon the importance of the present moment* when interpreting certain schools of philosophical and spiritual thought such as Platonism, Stoicism, and Epicureanism.

Here are a few excerpts from Hadot's essays that resonate well with some of our shared concerns, Kevin:

> Linked to the meditation upon death, the theme of the value of the present instant plays a fundamental role in all the philosophical schools. In short it is a consciousness of inner freedom. It can be summarized in a formula of this kind: you need only yourself in order immediately to find inner peace by ceasing to worry about the past and the future. You can be happy right now, or you will never be happy. Stoicism will insist on the effort needed to pay attention to oneself, the joyous acceptance of the present moment imposed on us by fate. The Epicurean will conceive of this liberation from cares about the past and the future as a relaxation, a pure joy of existing ... [83]

And here is another:

> Attention to the present moment is, in a sense, the key to spiritual exercises. It frees us from the passions, which are always caused by the past or the future – two areas which do *not* depend on us. By encouraging concentration on the minuscule present moment, which, in its exiguity, is always bearable and controllable, attention increases our vigilance. Finally, attention to the present moment allows us to accede to cosmic consciousness, by making us attentive to the infinite value of each instant, and causing us to accept each moment of existence from the viewpoint of the universal law of the *cosmos*.[84]

Many of the philosophies of spirituality that have interested me over the past several decades have centered upon the ineluctable importance of the present moment and around the dangers of forgetting or neglecting this significance. This perennial lesson, assisting us in the overcoming of nihilism, emerges continually throughout our attempts to interpret some of the central ideas of the great thinkers of both the East and the West, from Lao-tzu's concept of the Tao to Nietzsche's notion of the Eternal Recurrence of the Same to Jung's concept of synchronicity. Dürckheim, in fact, provides a wonderful transition for us in terms of bridging Eastern and Western thinkers, as we have seen.

KS: A spiritual appreciation of the creative moment and its potential for enriched meaningfulness are the hallmarks of human self-realization, then. The Self is not constrained by temporality, as Jung teaches us, but exists in an "Eternal Now." By exercising this way of thinking and experiencing, I take it, we may well find ourselves on the path to overcoming nihilism.

WG: This is a timeless or perennial lesson, just as the Self is timeless or perennial. Our aim, following Nietzsche's adoption of Pindar's maxim, is *to become what we truly are*. The study and application of Jungian psychology, viewed as a spiritual practice and way of life, helps us to understand more clearly this pursuit. Becoming what we truly are is not some task for the future, then. It is always a *challenge of the present moment*.

In keeping with this topic, I would now like to explore further the mystery of this connection between *self-realization* and *timelessness*. Dürckheim has helped us in this regard to bridge certain elements of Jung's psychology and the more existential aspects of Buddhism. Now I want to talk specifically about the parallels between Jung's thought and the spiritual philosophy of *Taoism*.

PART TWO

EXPLORING THE MYSTERY OF TIMELESSNESS: JUNG AND LAO-TZE

Prologue: "Crazy Time"

Kevin Stoehr: Bill, we have covered much ground since beginning our dialogue. Before turning directly to Jung and Taoism, let me review again. We have identified *the* spiritual problem of our times as nihilism, and outlined attempts at overcoming it through a renewed emphasis on spiritedness. Our discussion revolved mainly around the intersecting ideas of four thinkers who have had great influence in your many years of study of this problem. You have provided background on these thinkers and shown how their ideas and principles point to a richer and deeper conception of human selfhood than that offered by certain alternative viewpoints in Western philosophical and religious thinking.

Your studies of these topics and thinkers have been motivated by a deep devotion to the principle of the unity and wholeness of the human psyche and spirit. They have also been concerned with the loss of the sense of the meaning of "the One" and "the Whole," especially in the guise of nihilism since the time of Nietzsche.

I am most fascinated by the theme of *numinosity* and its connection with the topic of a *holistic and trans-personal Self.* This latter idea, as you have clearly pointed out, is presupposed by Nietzsche's idea of the Will to Power, by Jung's notion of the archetype of the Self, by Tillich's concept of Being-Itself, and by Dürkheim's category of Essential Being. These are also central themes in several Eastern philosophies and religions. And such a definition of selfhood seems to be a key to the overcoming of nihilism.

This unique conception of the relationships and connections that are inherent in the world and in our daily lives is very different, of course, from the traditional Aristotelian-Cartesian view of the universe as a vast aggregate of independent substances. Your holistic view of things also seems to depart dramatically from the tradition of linear thinking, in which causation is conceived as a series of causes and effects that are both linked and separated from one another by the rigid order of Time or Temporality. You have presented a different type of worldview, and one that is obviously needed, if I understand you correctly, in gaining a newfound appreciation for the principle of spiritedness in our daily lives.

You have stressed the idea of the emergence of a new spirituality, one that crosses boundaries between different world religions and one that overcomes merely conventional and collectivist notions of a transcendent deity. By focusing on these four thinkers, you have shown affinities in their writings concerning the equation of the Essential Self and "the God within," not to mention the affinities with certain Eastern ideas. And this pursuit of integrated wholeness involves openness to the experience of the numinous as well as an ability to recognize coincidences of opposites.

Would you now follow up on the idea of the numinous and timeless nature of trans-personal selfhood, Bill? Elaborate, if you will, on the holistic nature of this viewpoint and show how it involves our experience of numinosity and timelessness.

William Geoghegan: Well, let me start by saying that most of this can be explained clearly by focusing on Jung's notion of synchronicity or meaningful coincidence. On November 19, 1993, an article appeared on the Op-Ed page of *The New York Times*. It appeared a day before I was to deliver a lecture to the Jung Seminar on numinosity and synchronicity, so I regard my happening upon the article as a clear example in itself of synchronicity. It contained an excerpt by Carl Gustav Jung. That immediately grabbed my attention, of course. I also found that it summarized much of what I had prepared to say in my lecture. Let me read the article to you. It ran under the header "Crazy Times":

> The following is a previously unpublished letter, dated Nov. 12, 1959, from the psychologist C. G. Jung to Ruth Topping, a prominent Chicago social worker. She had asked him to explain a comment of his in a Chicago newspaper: "Among all my patients in the second half of life ... every one of them fell ill because he had lost what the living religions of every age have given their followers, and none of them has been really healed who did not regain his religious

outlook." In her letter, Miss Topping wondered how Jung would define the phrase "religious outlook."

By C. G. Jung, Zurich:

When you study the mental history of the world, you see that people since times immemorial had a general teaching or doctrine about the wholeness of the world. Originally and down to our days, they were considered to be holy traditions taught to the young people as a preparation for their future life. This has been the case in primitive tribes as well as in highly differentiated civilizations. The teaching had always a "philosophical" and "ethical" aspect.

In our civilization this spiritual background has gone astray. Our Christian doctrine has lost its grip to an appalling extent, chiefly because people don't understand it anymore. Thus one of the most important instinctual activities of our mind has lost its object.

As these views deal with the world as a whole, they create also a wholeness of the individual, so much so, that for instance a primitive tribe loses its vitality when it is deprived of its specific religious outlook. People are no more rooted in their world and lose their orientation. They just drift. That is very much our condition, too. The need for a meaning of their lives remains unanswered, because the rational, biological goals are unable to express the irrational wholeness of human life. Thus life loses its meaning. That is the problem of the "religious outlook" in a nutshell.

The problem itself cannot be settled by a few slogans. It demands concentrated attention, much mental work, and above all, patience, the rarest thing in our restless and crazy time.

KS: This does get to the heart of the matter, doesn't it? It reflects Jung's basic principle of individuation as a process of attaining a greater realization of selfhood or Self, in response to the contemporary problem of nihilism.

WG: Yes, and there is a clear parallel between his emphasis on "the wholeness of the world" and his emphasis on the wholeness of the psyche or Self. This is what we need to spell out in more detail. The experience of wholeness is that which occasions the concern with the numinous, with both the rational and non-rational aspects of our spiritual existence. And the recovery of our ultimate concern with our own wholeness leads us to the type of worldview that we have been hinting at. This is the worldview of the Taoist sage and of one who has come to see things in terms of the mutual arising of events and the interdependence of all beings.

KS: Why do you highlight the Taoist sage here, Bill? Surely there are other religions and philosophical schools that teach this holistic message. I think, for instance, of the Stoics and the Neo-Platonists and the Hindus.

WG: Indeed. It is a perennial and cross-cultural teaching, to be sure. As a parallel on the theological side I have been struck especially by Jean Pierre de Caussade's *L'Abandon à la providence divine* (1876), published in English as *The Sacrament of the Present Moment* (1921). My idea of spirituality, linked to that of Grace, is very much about crossing boundaries. But when teaching about this message of wholeness and its connection with the theme of numinosity, I think of the Taoist philosophy first, with its emphasis on the holistic and dialectical principle of the yin-yang relationship. I think of the Taoist sage and the clear way in which the sage provides a paradigm of the outward manifestation of this inner experience and insight. I think of the classic text of the *Tao Te Ching* which poetically conveys this teaching about the parallel wholeness of Self and World. And I think of Lao-tze, the legendary founder of Taoism, to whom Jung likened himself in reflecting on the great insights that he had absorbed over the course of his long life.

KS: I recall earlier connections that you have drawn between Jungian thought and the Taoist philosophy. Given that, Bill, let's travel down the pathway of the Tao, so to speak, to highlight this connection more clearly, especially as it relates to your view of our encounters with the numinous, timeless, and trans-personal Self.

Introduction: Holism and Numinosity

WG: It has been said that next to the Bible the *Tao Te Ching* is the most frequently translated book in the world. Most scholars believe that it took its present form about the fourth century BC, although some of its basic ideas go back much further. The title translates as the Treatise or Book of the Tao. "Tao" means "Way" – the way the universe really works – and "Te" refers to its virtue or excellence or power. I will say more about these terms later.

KS: I remember that I first read the *Tao Te Ching* in my senior year here at Bowdoin, when I assisted you with your course "Myth and Mysticism." At the time, it had a great effect on my way of thinking. I have also used this text in my own teaching. The *Tao Te Ching* is a book that is both philosophical *and* political at the same time, is it not?

WG: That's right. In general, the *Tao Te Ching* has a basic two-fold nature. Like the works of Confucius and his followers and some other schools of the time, it represents a spiritual response to the challenges of the anarchic, barbaric "Warring States Period" which lasted from approximately 850 to 221 BC, when China became a unified empire. In some respects, the *Tao Te Ching* is a practical treatise on political philosophy very broadly conceived, not altogether unlike Machiavelli's *The Prince*. More germane to our purpose is the fact that the *Tao Te Ching* is an archetypal expression of what is called "the perennial philosophy," referring to those basic principles which most world religions at their deepest contemplative level appear to have in common.

In China itself – although more than a few passages in the *Tao Te Ching* are quite critical of Confucianism – Taoism and Confucianism have much in common, such as the concept of Tao. And after Buddhism came to China around the first century, it blended with the two major indigenous traditions to form the "Three Religions." Thus Taoism, Confucianism, and Buddhism are not mutually exclusive as religions usually have been in the West. It should also be pointed out that in ancient China, like the West in antiquity, there was much less departmentalization of philosophy and religion as there has often been in the modern West.

KS: Talk for a moment about the relationship between Taoism and Buddhism.

WG: The relation between Taoism and Buddhism is especially interesting. The meditative form of Buddhism came to China about 500 AD and blended with Taoism to form Ch'an Buddhism. When Ch'an migrated to Japan, it was called "Zen." So basic elements of Taoism are also intrinsic to Zen. And, to take a huge jump over space, time, and many fundamental religious and cultural differences, we find today members in good standing of Roman Catholic religious orders who are also trained and ordained as Zen priests.

But to return to the *Tao Te Ching*: It consists of eighty-one literary units – chapters or poems – some long, some short, some clear, some obscure. Every time I read them I am reminded of Robert Frost's statement that "a poem is like a piece of ice that rides on its own melting." I can not imagine a book to which Frost's observation better applies.

KS: There is an ideogram for the Tao itself.

WG: Yes. The ideogram or picture-word for Tao is comprised of two characters, "head" and "walking man," which seems to imply a kind of dynamic, immanent teleology, a universal pattern, or a trans-personal cosmic purpose. "Te" means "to go straight to the heart of." The grand theme of the book is expressed in the Chinese term *tzu-jan*, meaning spontaneous or acting of its own accord. In contemporary terms, the universe of the *Tao Te Ching* is holistic: a living, self-regulating, organic system constantly tending toward homeostasis or vital equilibrium which it will maintain in the most appropriate way possible *if it is not interfered with*. The injunction, "Let all things take their natural course, and do not interfere," summarizes well the spirit of Taoism.[1]

As you inferred, it is not anachronistic to discern similarities between the *Tao Te Ching* and other holistic world perspectives. Nor do we need to fear "Westernizing" the *Tao Te Ching*. When we deal with Jung in relation to Taoism, for example, we see that, far from imposing his ideas upon it, Jung is himself influenced by Taoism at the deepest level of his existence, even to the point of finally identifying with its legendary founder, Lao-tze – the "old man" or "old boy."

In addition to Jung, I would like to mention the ideas of two other 20th century Western thinkers who can also illuminate the subject without distorting it.

The first is one we already know well: Rudolph Otto, with his famous idea of the holy or sacred as the numinous, the *mysterium tremendum et fascinans*, the tremendous and fascinating mystery, the infinitely awesome, the essence of the truly religious, mystical, and spiritual. Jung himself in his famous Terry Lectures at Yale identifies the essential quality of his central concept of the Collective or Universal Unconscious (the "objective psyche") as the numinous.[2]

One question, then, is the following: What form does the numinous take in the *Tao Te Ching*? This is crucial since we are comparing Taoism with Jung's experience and discovering where the elements of dramatic, cataclysmic, tremendous and fascinating mystery are quite strong. We shall find that the *tremendum* or awe-inspiring and sometimes terrifying element of the numinous is present in the *Tao Te Ching*, as well as in the older Jung, in a very subtle but nonetheless telling manner.

R. C. Zaehner, who was the Spalding Professor of Eastern Religions and Ethics at Oxford until his death in 1974, one of the two or three top scholars of religion in the world. In his recent book *Jung and the Outside World*, Barry Ulanov makes the point that Jung's greatest influence on the world outside of psychology was upon scholarship in comparative religion, and the figure by whom Zaehner was most influenced was Jung. Some years ago Zaehner published a famous essay, entitled "A New Buddha and A New Tao", in which he claimed that two new religions were going to captivate and dominate the world in the coming century. The first was Marxism, on which the jury is still out in some quarters, and the second was Jungianism. He called Jung the "new Buddha," but I believe he would have done better to call him the "new Lao-tze," as I shall discuss later.

I also cite Zaehner because he provides a much used three-fold classification of philosophical and religious mysticism: (1) natural mysticism, focused on the living world of Nature; (2) theistic mysticism, focused on a personal God; and (3) monistic mysticism, focused on a transcendental primal unity.[3] The *Tao Te Ching* is a prime example of a form of mystical spirituality in which the numinous is mediated by the impersonal and pluralistic processes of the natural world, as we shall see when we look at its texts. I'll turn now to consider the *Tao Te Ching*, as much as possible in its own words. I will use here the fine translation by the poet Stephen Mitchell.

The Paradoxical and Holistic Nature of the Tao

KS: How do you normally go about teaching the *Tao Te Ching*? I recall that you covered several central themes when you taught that text to freshmen and sophomore students many years ago.

WG: That's correct. I always deal with four major themes in the *Tao Te Ching*: (1) *Tao* (Way), (2) *Yin-Yang*, (3) *Shih* (or Sage), and (4) *Te* (Virtue). In reality these themes cannot be compartmentalized and segregated, although they may be dealt with serially for purposes of exposition.

Taoism stands for what Thich Nhat Hanh, the Vietnamese Buddhist monk, calls "inter-being," in contrast to a traditionally Western and especially Aristotelian concept of a being or a reality as "any entity capable of *independent* existence." In Taoism nothing exists independently; all exists inter-dependently. The Taoist sage may *behave* independently, as *pu shih*, as one having "independent integrity," but he *exists* as an integral part of a subtly and complexly interwoven whole. This Taoist view is echoed in Jung's comment about himself that "the difference between me and most people is that for me the dividing walls between things are transparent."

So, with focus upon inter-being or wholeness, let us turn to consider the first two lines of Poem #56, perhaps the best known words in the *Tao Te Ching*: "Those who know don't talk. / Those who talk don't know."[4] The theme is the irreducible mystery of Tao. Tao is not a problem that can, even in principle, ever be solved. Its mystery will never be *comprehended*, although it may be *apprehended* intuitively and directly. Inutterability is the basic meaning of *mystery* and *mysticism*, which both are derived from the Greek word *muo*, meaning "to be silent."

As the influential 20th century philosopher Ludwig Wittgenstein put it at the conclusion of his famous *Tractatus Logico-philosophicus*: "*Wovon man nicht sprechen kann, darüber muss man schweigen*," or "Whereof one cannot speak, thereof one must be silent."[5] He also wrote: "There is indeed the inexpressible. This shows itself; it is the mystical."[6] What cannot be said can only be *shown*.

KS: I see the *Tao Te Ching* as embodying the same paradox that constitutes Wittgenstein's *Tractatus*. It uses language to point to that which cannot be expressed in language, and at the same time recognizes this ineffability.

WG: That is a very good parallel. The mystical is the unsayable. We can only point to it indirectly and metaphorically. And the mystical is related directly to the numinous. I would see the *Tao Te Ching* as a prime illustration of the philosopher Martin Heidegger's assertion that "the most extreme sharpness and depth of thought belongs to all genuine and great mysticism."[7] Consideration of the paradoxical requires rigorous thought, not lazy speculation. The paradoxical and the mystical present us with *questions to be lived,* as Rilke put it.

The theme of paradox is quite apparent in Poem #41, which shows us that ultimate mystery expresses itself in paradox. It begins: "Thus it is said:/ the path into the light seems dark,/ the path forward seems to go back."[8]

KS: This theme of paradox, when treating the mystical or the numinous, recalls our earlier theme of a coincidence of opposites: Hegel's Dialectic, Otto's *mysterium tremendum et fascinans*, and Tillich's notion of finite freedom.

WG: Yes, and the best-known of all Taoist paradoxes is the principle of *wei wu wei*, meaning literally "act not act," usually translated as "non-action," the ideogram of which is "forty men disappear into the forest." Poem #37 captures this paradoxical notion of "acting by not acting," usually translated simply as "non-action": "The Tao never does anything, / yet through it all things are done."[9]

Jung himself translated *wei wu wei* as "doing nothing but also not doing nothing," and the comparative religion scholar Huston Smith translates it as "The way to *do* is to *be*." I am tempted to suggest that the best idiomatic translation would be, "If it ain't broke, don't fix it." Or as younger people used to say: "Go with the flow." We are speaking here of a form of action which is uncontrived and which involves a large measure of acceptance of the way that things happen to be in the present moment. The Stoics, as we had mentioned earlier, speak of *Amor fati* or "love of fate." I am reminded also of Pindar's maxim that we have also mentioned, "Become what you are," echoed by the Nietzschean "letting beings be and become." The notion of *wu wei* is explicit or implicit in almost every poem of the book. It captures the paradoxicality of the Tao itself and it is related to the famous complementarity of Yin and Yang.

The Complementarity of *Yin* and *Yang*

WG: The holistic interconnection of all things is expressed in the first verse of Poem #42: "The Tao gives birth to One. / One gives birth to Two. / Two gives birth to Three. / Three gives birth to all things."[10] This verse expresses Taoist cosmogony or vision of world-creation. Everything and everyone has its source in the Tao. The second verse of the poem expresses complementarity: "When male and female combine, / all things achieve harmony."[11]

The principle of the complementarity of Yin and Yang is expressed in a well-known symbol that often serves as the logo for Tao and Taoism, the Diagram of the Great Ultimate. As Fritjof Capra has noted in his *The Tao of Physics*, there is a dynamic symmetry to the diagram in which the darker *yin* and brighter *yang* are perpetually rotating and revolving, giving place to one another as moments of a whole unity. And furthermore, the *yin* aspect of the whole contains an element or hint of the *yang* aspect, and vice-versa. The darker element contains a trace of the lighter element, and the reverse also holds. These seeming opposites are really complementary and their dynamic, dialectical relationship points to an integrated form of wholeness that includes them.[12]

This eternal cyclical process expressed by the Diagram of the Great Ultimate is referred to in the *Tao Te Ching* as "return" or "reversion."

KS: Jung has a similar notion, doesn't he?

WG: He does.   Jung frequently refers to the same idea as *enantiodromia*, a term borrowed from his much-admired Heraclitus, meaning "running contrariwise."   Jung defines "enantiodromia" as "conversion," or "transformation into the opposite," and sees it as the fundamental pattern of the automatic compensatory behavior of the psyche.   Certain aspects of the human personality instinctually compensate for other aspects.   Positive psychological energy compensates for negative psychological energy, and vice-versa. This is shown clearly by Jung's notion of the "shadow personality."

KS: Herb Coursen, your former colleague here at Bowdoin and my former professor of literature, explains this theme of psychological complementarity through a Jungian interpretation of different Shakespearean characters in his book *The Compensatory Psyche*.[13] He points there, for instance, to the complementarity of the feminine and masculine within certain literary characters, what Jung calls the relationship between the *anima* and the *animus* within every human personality.

WG: That's right. The principle of the complementarity of the transpersonal feminine and masculine interactive energy modes of Yin and Yang also illustrates the principle of the unity or coincidence of opposites, as you had suggested. This is the paradoxical nature of the mystical or the numinous that was mentioned earlier. But there is really a paradox only if one does not grasp fully the underlying idea of complementarity. This is a standard theme of the perennial philosophy and an ingredient of the mysticism of most world religions. Incidentally, it is also expressed in quantum physics, as in the Nobel Laureate Niels Bohr's principle of complementarity, illustrated in the *yin-yang* symbolism of his coat-of-arms with its motto *contraria sunt complementa*, "contraries are complementary." But more on Bohr later.

And so Yin and Yang are often described as ancient archetypal expressions of the trans-personal feminine and masculine, akin to Jung's anima and animus, but the issue for Lao-tze as a philosopher is not primarily gender differentiation but the universal and necessary complementarity of Being and Non-Being. Consider Poem #11, which we quoted earlier when speaking of Karlfried Graf Dürckheim's transformational encounter with these words. This poem emphasizes the "emptiness" and "non-being" that gives something its use and meaning.

KS: As I remember, it was this poem that had a striking effect on the architect Frank Lloyd Wright. I recall from his writings that he first happened upon this poem after becoming highly interested in the art and cultures of the East and after having already formulated his basic architectural philosophy. His theory of organic architecture revolves around the principle that *space* or *emptiness* is the essence of architecture, rather than the building materials that frame a certain space. When he hit upon the poem, he was apparently thunderstruck that the same insight had been emphasized by Lao-tze over two thousand years before.[14] The poem also makes me think of Martin Heidegger's essay "The Thing" ("*Das Ding*"), where he emphasizes the empty space of a jug as being the vessel's essential "element" or "quality." [15] For Heidegger, emptiness or Non-Being can create a "clearing" for the arising of something useful or meaningful or significant.

WG: Those are very apt parallels here. The fundamental insight that lies behind this poem of the *Tao Te Ching* – with its homely, everyday illustrations of the complementarity of the actuality of Being and the potentiality of Non-Being – precipitated in the person of Karlfried Graf Dürckheim, whom we have discussed. As I have noted, Dürckheim introduced the notion of "the shock of Non-Being." This was essential in what he calls "initiation into Being," his realization of the unity of all apparent opposites, especially the "inner" and the "outer," the subjective and the objective. We shall see that something very similar takes place in Jung's experience.

KS: How does all of this relate to the principle of *wei wu wei*, "acting by not acting?"

WG: Well, I'll try to get to the essence of the matter here. Using the imagery of the poem, it is the center hole, the center *wu*, the center emptiness, the center Non-Being, the center death, that is a metaphor for the psychological experience of the Self, a decisive relativization of self-defeating, self-destructive ego-centricity and ego-inflation, to put it in Jungian terms. It is the ego or conscious "I" that, when over-emphasized, leads to a feeling of alienation or estrangement from others and even from Nature itself.

KS: So the Taoist message here is one of a trans-personal unity of opposites that is expressed most essentially by the wholeness of the Self. This includes the unity of masculine and feminine, for example, as well as the unity of our conscious and unconscious selves. But the *Tao Te Ching* puts more emphasis on the *feminine* aspect of the personality, doesn't it? I would think that this emphasis detracts a bit from the overall lesson about wholeness.

WG: In its own milieu and in its subsequent history, the *Tao Te Ching* stands out for its emphasis upon the Yin, the trans-personal feminine dimension of reality. The feminine principle of Yin may be said to represent the aspects of Non-Being or Potentiality within the cyclical and cosmic motion of the Tao. But this does not detract from the lesson about wholeness. It is precisely the aspect of Non-Being or Potentiality that needs to be emphasized, since it is so often overlooked as constitutive of psychological reality. This is shown in Poem #28:

> The world is formed from the void,
> like utensils from a block of wood.
> The Master knows the utensils,
> yet keeps to the block:
> thus she can use all things.[16]

Especially significant here is the concept of the "block," also translated as "the uncarved block," *p'o*, meaning pure potentiality. Incidentally, Mao Tze-tung in his *Little Red Book* referred to the Chinese people as "p'o," translated as "poor and blank," like a sheet of paper upon which he would write its future history. The political implication is obvious, but I think that the primary Taoist meaning of Yin, the valley spirit, and the uncarved block is that of *pure potentiality* – as when Heidegger, in an arresting phrase, speaks of the "silent power of the possible."

KS: And enacting the principle of *wei wu wei* is similar to returning to the state of the uncarved block?

WG: Precisely. I'd now like to examine the character of the Taoist sage, the *Tao-Shih*, as one who leads by returning to "the state of the uncarved block." This is an individual who acts by not acting, one who lives by the principle of *wei wu wei* and who thereby actualizes his potential to a fitting degree.

The *Tao-Shih* and *Te*

KS: How then would you describe the character of the Taoist sage who is also a leader, who must somehow be both active and passive simultaneously?

WG: A *Tao-shih* is a practitioner of Tao. This term has been variously translated as leader, master, prince, king, ideal human, authentic existent, evolved individual and individuated or individuating person. I prefer "sage" because it perhaps best expresses the notion of Taoism as a wisdom teaching. The sage is a naturally graced person who embodies Tao, its mystery, its paradoxes and complementarities, and above all, *wei wu wei*. Dürckheim writes, "Those who follow the way become the way."

When I think of the sage I think of the Japanese term *sabi*, meaning solitude, and of Whitehead's definition of religion itself as "what an individual does with his own solitariness." The cardinal virtue of the sage, consonant with *wu wei*, is his humility, because that is the way of the Tao which, like water, the weakest of all things, in the end overcomes all. The most vivid word-picture of the sage is found in Poem #15. There the "ancient Master" is described as "someone crossing an iced-over stream./ Alert as a warrior in enemy territory./ Courteous as a guest./ Fluid as melting ice./ Shapable as a block of wood./ Receptive as a valley./ Clear as a glass of water."[17]

So the Taoist idea of "the master" involves self-acceptance and the acceptance of all things. And we see in Poem #22 how the paradoxical or complementary nature of Tao is expressed in the conduct of sages. This poem is especially relevant to our prior theme of self-realization and the pursuit of the wholeness of the human personality. It begins: "If you want to become whole,/ let yourself be partial./ If you want to become straight,/ let yourself be crooked."[18]

We should take special note of the final two lines of this poem: "Only in being lived by the Tao / can you be truly yourself." That, of course, is really what it is all about, everything that we have been discussing: being truly yourself and knowing your Self truly.

In Poem #12, we come to understand that the sage is guided by his emotive intelligence: "The Master observes the world / but trusts his inner vision."[19] These lines tell us how the sage knows. *If* one were to type-test him according to Jungian psychological typology, he might turn out to be an INFP: an introverted, intuitive, feeling perceiver, whose anti-type, or shadow, would be an ESTJ, an extroverted, sensing, judging thinker. Since it has been estimated that some seventy-five per cent of the American people are ESTJ's, it is unlikely that Taoism will sweep the country. Nevertheless, ESTJ's might well consider seasoning their psyches with the wisdom of those two crucial lines in Mitchell's translation. Again: "The Master observes the world/ but trusts his inner vision." We see in Mitchell's translation a recurrence of the primal unity of opposites – in this case the coincidence of interior and exterior existence, of subjectivity and objectivity. The orientation of the *Tao Te Ching* is toward the external expression of inner virtue and power – what is called *Te* – of the Tao in this world and in everyday life.

KS: Say a bit more about *Te*. It sounds something like what the ancient Greeks called *arete* as their term for virtue or functional excellence.

WG: Yes, and Greek philosophers such as Socrates and Plato and Aristotle were also concerned with the outer manifestation of inner power or moral virtue. In Poem #54 we witness a progressive, holistic, and logical chain extending from an individual wisdom ethic to basic principles of public policy and then to the idea of cosmic harmony. It is here that we begin to see the great parallel between the shared goals of Taoism: wholeness of Self, wholeness of Society, and wholeness of the World. Poem #54 asks: "How do I know this is true?" The answer: "By looking inside myself."[20]   In this connection I think also of economist Glenn Loury's suggestion for beginning to remedy the problems of America's inner city minorities: "One by one and from the inside out," as the title of his book proposes.

This poem parallels, quite synchronistically, the then-contemporary Western Stoic wisdom of living "agreeably with nature," so as to become a "citizen of the cosmopolis," the whole, the universe itself, as we find in Epictetus among others.

The Taoist ideal or timeless state of mind or spirit is suggestive of the Japanese *wabi*, meaning naturalness or rustic unpretentiousness. It seems to me that anyone familiar with the life and thought of Jung will sense the kind of deep spiritual affinity – transcending space, time, and cultural differences – between the sage of Bollingen and the solitariness and rusticity beloved of Lao-tze, the legendary author of the *Tao Te Ching*.

Meaning, Meditation, and Synchronicity in Taoism and Jung

KS: The foregoing has provided a basic sense of how you understand the Taoist sage and the basic Taoist principles of the Tao, *Te*, and *wei wu wei*. As you have just suggested by your comments, it would be good to have you talk more specifically now about the connections between Taoist holism and the thought of Jung.

WG: What I want to suggest is that Taoism – the spirit of Tao – was not only influential upon Jung, as were many other currents of thought, but *decisive, determinative,* and *consummatory* of his basic orientation. In making this point, I would like to turn now to the *meditative* aspect of Taoism and to link this with Jung's notion of synchronicity, which parallels the Taoist notion of "interdependent being" or "inter-being," a holistic perspective on oneself and one's place in the cosmos.

One might summarize all that I have to say in the following way: *Meaning is the message and meditation is the method.* That in itself signalizes a truly profound affinity, at least in my opinion, between Jung and Taoism. One might say that the Tao could be characterized as *meaning* in terms of a *deep interconnectedness,* an *organic harmony,* and a *mysterious merging,* which are terms used in respect to the Tao in the *Tao Te Ching.*

Richard Wilhelm, a great friend of Jung, translated not only *The Secret of the Golden Flower* but also the *I Ching* and the *Tao Te Ching.* The term which Wilhelm used for the Tao is the German term "Sinn," meaning *meaning.* So here is Wilhelm, expert in the Chinese language and literature and life in China, who uses the term "meaning" to translate "Tao."[21]   The key to meditation for Wilhelm and other scholars who have studied the subject is *wu wei,* which we now know as non-action or, as Jung puts it, "doing nothing but also not doing nothing." *Wu wei* is the keynote, so to speak, of Taoist meditation.

Now, the parallel in Jung to Tao is Self. That point is stated by Jung himself. The term for the form of meditation that Jung really created is "active imagination," which we have discussed earlier in our dialogue When we are talking about the deep connection between Taoism and Jung, the principle of synchronicity must be brought in here as Jung's term for the kind of multiple interdependent causality that is characteristic of Chinese thought and also Buddhist and Hindu thought. This involves the notion of "mutual arising," so that there is a holistic rather than linear explanation for everything that happens.

KS: You emphasize meditation here. As I understand it, the Bowdoin Jung Seminar that you founded has not only focused on Jungian dream interpretation and the interpretation of various texts by Jung, but has also undertaken studies of various forms of spiritual meditation.

WG: Yes, and all of that is interconnected, as I'm attempting to point out here. In fact, I would like to refer briefly here to three other recent lectures on meditation presented at the Seminar. One of those lectures was "Meditation Mandala" by Walter Christie, who has served for many years as a psychiatrist at the Maine Medical Center and who has also taught psychiatry. The one thing that I would like to lift out of that lecture is his emphasis on the *via negativa* or negative way in mysticism, which is expressed as *wu wei* in Taoism.

Christie used the term "negative capability," referring to the use of that term by the poet John Keats. Keats referred to Shakespeare as possessing "negative capability," which I think is an extraordinary term that applies very definitely to Jung's active imagination and to *wu wei*. This is the way that Keats defined "negative capability": the capability of "being in uncertainty, mysteries, doubts, without any irritable reaching after fact and reason."[22] There is nothing wrong, so far as Shakespeare is concerned, with fact and reason, but the irritable straining is the fly in the ointment. And that is where the patience, the waiting, the quality of endurance of *wu wei* comes in: the *Geschehenlassen*, the letting or allowing something to happen, which is the prime ingredient of Jung's notion of active imagination and Nietzsche's idea of the Eternal Recurrence as a type of *amor fati* or love of fate.

KS: Earlier I referred to an essay by Heidegger, "The Thing." I also recall a question that Heidegger poses in another essay, "The Origin of the Work of Art": "What seems easier than to let a being be just the being that it is?"[23] And the title of his later philosophical dialogue on meditative thinking, *Gelassenheit*, suggests an attitude of "release" or "letting-be."

WG: That's precisely the idea, the Nietzschean maxim of "letting be and become," as we might formulate his synthesis of being and becoming. In another lecture, my long-time associate, Jungian analyst

Paul Huss, dealt with the meditation complex. The idea here is that not only is the ego (along with a number of other things) an autonomous psychological entity in the make-up of an individual or of the collective species, but that meditation itself can be a complex, an autonomous psychological entity in one's thinking, feeling, and behavior. This happens when meditation develops into the form of a complex that can benignly serve as an intermediary between the ego and the ultimate concern of the ego. The ultimate concern of the ego is the ultimate meaning of the ego's existence – namely, the Self, what Jung calls "das Selbst," "the itself," which is equivalent to the Tao or even to the Western conception of God, or to the Buddha nature, or to the Hindu Brahman. [24]

Finally, I would like to mention an idea from my friend Chris Beach's talk about meditation and from his own background and training as a Jungian analyst. The idea is also based on his own real-life experience: meditation as active imagination is not just a hobby to be taken up to while away the time, but it is a matter of life and death. It certainly was for Jung, indeed a matter of life and death biologically and in terms of the meaning of his own existence. I think that it evokes Paul Tillich's concept of "ultimate concern." Tillich sees ultimate concern as the quintessence of all serious religions and all serious philosophies. What they all deal with, as Tillich puts it, is *was uns unbedingt angeht*, that which concerns us unconditionally or ultimately. And unless we deal with that which concerns us ultimately, we are not really being serious.

KS: How does this understanding of the importance of meditation, as connected with the Taoist ethic of *wei wu wei* or uncontrived action, relate to the holism and trans-personal reality that is involved in Tao and in Jung's idea of synchronicity?

WG: Among other things, meditation is an openness toward the holistic nature of things. Jung defines *synchronicity*, as I have earlier remarked, as meaningful coincidence, as an acausal or non-linear principle of explanation or understanding. He worked on that concept with the well-known quantum physicist Wolfgang Pauli, who was a client and friend and professional associate of Jung. I'd like to return to the relationship between Jung and Pauli a bit later, also in connection with Bohr, whom I have mentioned when remarking on the parallel between Jung's thoughts on psychological complementarity and Bohr's emphasis upon that principle in quantum theory. The principles of complementarity and synchronicity are closely related to our familiar principles of self-realization and integrated wholeness. The general lesson here is, as we have noted, a *dialectical* one, recalling Hegel. At the end of the day, we cannot maintain any view of the Self or of the World that presupposes absolute divisions or absolute oppositions. There is a primordial, underlying unity that must always be recognized.

Now I want to give an example of synchronicity. Let me begin with the following anecdote as recounted by Jung's biographer, Barbara Hannah. One of Jung's many friends in the field of comparative religion was the Sinologist Richard Wilhelm, who told Jung a story illustrating better than anything else the absolute priority he accorded to the spiritual life. The story is called "The Fable of the Rainmaker." Hannah adds that Jung advised her always to include the story in any course of lectures she gave, and that Jung himself told the story repeatedly right up until the end of his active life. It goes as follows:

> Richard Wilhelm was in a remote Chinese village which was suffering from a most unusually prolonged drought. Everything had been done to put an end to it, and every kind of prayer and charm had been used, but all to no avail. So the elders of the village told Wilhelm that the only thing to do was to send for a rainmaker from a distance. This interested him enormously and he was careful to be present when the rainmaker arrived. He came in a covered cart, a small, wizened old man. He got out of the cart, sniffed the air in distaste, then asked for a cottage on the outskirts of the village. He made the condition that no one should disturb him and that his food should be put down outside the door. Nothing was heard of him for three days; then everyone woke up to a downpour of rain. It even snowed, which was unknown at that time of year.
>
> Wilhelm was greatly impressed and sought out the rainmaker, who had now come out of his seclusion. Wilhelm asked him in wonder: "So you can make rain?" The old man scoffed at the very idea and said *of course* he could not. "But there was the most persistent drought until you came," Wilhelm retorted, "and then – within three days – it rains?" "Oh," replied the old man, "that was something quite different. You see, I come from a region where everything is in order, it rains when it should and is fine when that is needed, and the people also are in order and in themselves. But that was not the case with the people here, they were all out of Tao and out of themselves. I was at once infected when I arrived, so I had to be quite alone until I was once more in Tao and then naturally it rained!" [25]

KS: That's a wonderful little fable.

WG: Yes, it is. This story is an excellent parabolic illustration of *wei wu wei* which, you will recall, Jung translates as "doing nothing but also not doing nothing." It is also a superb example of synchronicity, that acausal principle of explanation and understanding which parallels the holistic notion of Tao as ground and essence of interdependent existence or "inter-being," a cosmic interweaving of events.

This parable of synchronicity informs us that whatever we do with our minds affects our bodies, and whatever affects our bodies affects our minds. And whatever we do affects our view of the world, and our view of the world affects the world in which we live, and the world in which we live affects the world in which everybody lives. So there's a holistic logic to the fable here that is irrefutable. Now the Chinese put the point in this way, as we find in the *Tao Te Ching*: "Sageliness within, kingliness without." This returns us to our earlier point about Jungian synchronicity and the holistic unity of opposites that is afforded by the notion of the Tao: a correlation of the inner and the outer.

We should also remember here again Jung's description of the Self as "the God within," as an "incorruptible value," as the "irruption of the imperishable into the transitory."[26] He also explicitly identifies Self with the Tao and with the Center. Erich Neumann, whom Jung regarded as the most able of his disciples, refers to the individuation process as something transcending both introversion and extroversion (those two fundamental personality orientations which Jung identified), which Neumann calls most aptly "centroversion," turning to the center which is the Self or the Tao.[27] And again, we recall here the Taoist sage as one who expresses inner virtue or power in his outer daily life.

Let us turn now to Jung's own words about the central purpose of his life – his vocation, his mission – and then consider how that relates to both synchronicity and Taoism. He writes in *Memories, Dreams, Reflections*: "My life has been permeated and held together by one idea and one goal: namely, to penetrate into the secret of the personality. Everything can be explained from this central point, and all my works relate to this one theme."[28] I can hardly imagine a more unequivocal statement. Jung wrote this in his maturity after his harrowing, numinous "Confrontation with the Unconscious" during World War I. But he also documented his earlier concern with "the secret of the personality" as a boy who, in his reflections, echoes a famous Taoist story. This may well be taken as yet another example of synchronicity. The eight-year-old Jung was playing in the garden of his parents' home. Here are Jung's own words:

> In front of this wall was a slope in which was embedded a stone that jutted out – my stone. Often, when I was alone, I sat down on this stone, and then began an imaginary game that went something like this: "I am sitting on top of this stone and it is underneath." But the stone also could say "I" and think: "I am lying here on this slope and he is sitting on top of me." The question then arose: "Am I the one who is sitting on the stone, or am I the stone on which *he* is sitting?" This question always perplexed me, and I would stand up, wondering who was what now. The answer remained totally unclear, and my uncertainty was accompanied by a feeling of curious and fascinating darkness. But there was no doubt whatsoever that this stone stood in some secret relationship to me. I could sit on it for hours, fascinated by the puzzle it set me.[29]

Although Jung was not aware of it at the time, this experience with the stone provides a wonderful incident of synchronicity in that it parallels a famous dream by Chuang-tzu, considered the greatest of Lao-tze's later disciples. Chuang-tzu dreamt that he was a butterfly and, upon awakening, did not know whether he had been dreaming that he was butterfly or whether he was now a butterfly dreaming that he was a man.

The parallel between the boy-stone and the man-butterfly relationships seems to indicate that from this early stage of evolving consciousness, Jung was a kind of natural Taoist. As he writes in the very next paragraph after the re-telling of this boyhood incident, he returned to the scene of his boyhood experience many years after his life-changing confrontation with the Unconscious in which he discovered through personal experience the meditative method of active imagination as the path to individuation. The attraction of the recollection of the *timelessness* of that early experience was so strong that he had to pull himself away by reminding himself of his familial and professional responsibilities. Yes, here's the passage. Jung writes:

> Thirty years later I again stood on that slope. I was a married man, had children, a house, a place in the world, and a head full of ideas and plans, and suddenly I was again the child who had kindled a fire full of secret significance and sat down on the stone without knowing whether it was I or I was it. I thought suddenly of my life in Zürich, and it seemed alien to me, like news from some remote world and time. This was frightening, for the world of my childhood in which I

had just become absorbed was *eternal*, and I had been wrenched away from it and had fallen into a time that continued to roll onward, moving farther and farther away. The pull of that other world was so strong that I had to tear myself violently from the spot in order not to lose hold of my future.[30]

Jung is writing of a period when he was thirty-eight or thirty-nine, just after he emerged from his "rock-bottom" mid-life crisis, to use his own term. Of that emergence he says that he "began to understand that the goal of psychic development is the self. There is no linear evolution: there is only a circumambulation of the self ... I knew that in finding the mandala as an expression of the self I had attained what was for me the ultimate."[31]

Shortly after these reflections upon his boyhood experience, in 1927, Jung had a mandala dream which was for him determinative of his future life-course. This dream, set in Liverpool, was highly representative of the acausal and holistic principle of synchronicity. He writes of the great insight afforded by that dream:

One could not go beyond the center. The center is the goal, and everything is directed toward that center. Through this dream I understood that the self is the principle and archetype of orientation and meaning. Therein lies its healing function.[32]

A year later, in 1928, when Jung was painting the mandala of "The Castle," he received from Richard Wilhelm a copy of *The Secret of the Golden Flower*, an ancient Taoist alchemical treatise. Wilhelm asked him to provide a psychological commentary on the Golden Flower, which itself was a mandalic representation of Tao.

KS: What is it precisely that Jung discovered at this time?

WG: Jung had discovered in his own direct psychological experience the circular *mandala* as the symbol par excellence of the Self, the deep center, the principle of unity, totality, and ultimate meaning in the human personality, which he was later to call "the God within." This discovery had two very important implications for Jung.

Primary is the fact that it was the first, and for a time the only, analogue that Jung could find to illustrate his own numinous experience of the Self as the resolution of his disintegrative spiritual crisis. The Gnostic material into which he had looked – and to which he had contributed in his *Seven Sermons to the Dead* (*Septem Sermones ad*

Mortuos), written during the crisis – would not do because it did not reflect sufficiently direct personal experience of the eternal, the "always-so," as the *Tao Te Ching* puts it. He needed a more effective way to point to the reality of the Self as the integrated wholeness of the psyche. The mandala symbolized both synchronicity and numinosity, crucial elements of this overall insight.

In the second place, the fact that *The Secret of the Golden Flower* was an alchemical treatise gave Jung a breakthrough insight. He realized that, in the West, alchemy was the link between the ancient Gnostics and his own discovery and conceptualization of the Collective Unconscious or objective psyche, what we might call the universality of human psychological experience.

In addition, Jung observes that the first book that he published after his emergence from his mid-life crisis was *Psychological Types*. He writes that it "yielded the insight that every judgment made by an individual is conditioned by his personality type and that every point of view is necessarily relative. This raised the question of the unity which must compensate for this diversity, and it led me directly to the Chinese concept of the Tao."[33]   Note the phrase "unity which must compensate for this diversity." Again, this is the holistic message that we have been considering right along.

So all of this concerns the activity of crossing cultural boundaries and the key role that Jungian thought is playing in that. One of the things that just struck me recently is the fact that, because Zen Buddhism is comprised of both Taoism and Buddhist ideas, wherever you find Zen, you can find Taoism and the Tao. The Buddhists themselves say – and this is extraordinarily significant – that Zen can be detached from Buddhism, detached from any religion, from any philosophy, indeed from anything, and at the same time can identify with anything. In other words, Zen – derived from a Sanskrit term meaning "certitude emerging from meditation" – is *universalizable*, which would imply in an indirect way that the fundamental principles of Jung are universalizable in the same way that Zen is, given the deep parallels that we have discussed. I think this is truly extraordinary and may well be – turning out according to the Tao, so to speak – that the greatest contributions of Jung are going to be along these lines, transcending his metier of psychotherapy.

Tao as Self and Jung as "A New Lao-tzu"

KS: Earlier you spoke of Jung as a "new Lao-tze."

WG: Indeed. Not only is Tao a determinative symbol for Jung's central concept of the Self, but Lao-tze himself is the model for Jung's final appraisal of the meaning of his existence. First, let me quote Poem #20 of the *Tao Te Ching*, which is highly relevant for this comparison. Lao-tzu tells us there: "Other people are bright; /I alone am dark./... I drift like a wave on the ocean,/ I blow as aimless as the wind."[34] Now let me read the final paragraph of Jung's *Memories, Dreams, Reflections*. These are among the last words he ever wrote for publication:

> When Lao-tzu says "All are clear, I alone am clouded," he is expressing what I now feel in advanced old age. Lao-tzu is the example of a man with superior insight who has seen and experienced worth and worthlessness, and who at the end of his life desires to return into his own being, into the eternal unknowable meaning. The archetype of the old man who has seen enough is eternally true. At every level of intelligence this type appears, and its lineaments are always the same, whether it be an old peasant or a great philosopher like Lao-tzu. This is old age, and a limitation. Yet there is so much that fills me: plants, animals, clouds, day and night, and the eternal in man. The more uncertain I have felt about myself, the more there has grown up in me a feeling of kinship with all things. In fact it seems to me as if that alienation which so long separated me from the world has become transferred into my own inner world, and has revealed to me an unexpected unfamiliarity with myself.[35]

Let us remember that these are the words of a man who had throughout his life a powerful sense of the uniqueness of every individual personality, not least his own. Let me quote the last sentence again: "In fact it seems to me as if that alienation which so long separated me from the world has become transformed into my own inner world, and has revealed to me an unexpected unfamiliarity with myself." Here the numinous, the *mysterium tremendum et fascinans*, is experienced quietly as a consummatory inner event.

KS: How do you interpret Jung's self-reflection here?

WG: This is the ego's discovery of the Self. What Jung is saying, it seems to me, is that that which was formerly without, the Other, is now experienced as within, also his very Self, just as the stone was to the boy of eight. The infinite is within. God or the Self is within. As St. Augustine says when addressing God in his *Confessions*, "But you were more inward than my most inward part and higher than the highest element in me."[36]

Thus Jung, having learned through the hard way of his mid-life crisis to look within – to *really* look, as if his life and sanity depended upon it, which they did – had like Lao-tze long before him learned to look without the way he had looked within. In other words, towards the very end of his life, Jung begins to develop the concept of what he called *unus mundus*, that is to say, the world conceived as a unity.[37] And that is precisely the holistic vision of interdependent existence that is emphasized in Taoism.

KS: Well, you've brought me a long way with all of this, Bill. As far as this connection between Jung's thought and Taoism is concerned, could you summarize some of the basic points that you have made?

WG: I can certainly try. Throughout his mature life Jung indicated that his ultimate concern was with the deep unity underlying the bewildering diversities of existence. He sometimes used the Sanskrit term *nirdvandva*, meaning non-dual, to signify this transcendental unity. He railed against what he called the "box-system" of conventional thinking, and found, as we have seen, "the dividing walls between things to be transparent." His thought culminates in his central concept of *individuation*, which itself is derived from the Latin "individuum," the undivided.

Jung emphasizes the complementarity of individual uniqueness and of universality in the life-long individuation process. He writes that such complementarity means "coming to selfhood" or "self-realization" as a unique whole that, however, is the opposite of the "ego-centeredness and autoeroticism" with which self-realization is all too frequently confused. It points to a trans-personal holism, such as is expressed by experiences of synchronicity. Furthermore, let me read a quick quote from his Glossary at the end of *Memories, Dreams, Reflections*. He adds that "the self comprises infinitely more than a mere ego ... It is as much one's self, and all other selves, as the ego.

Individuation does not shut one out from the world, but gathers the world to oneself."[38]

In this way, with powerful assistance from Taoism, Jung fulfilled his vocational vow to "penetrate the secret of the personality." He, like Lao-tze and many others before him, penetrated it and discovered that the core of the personality – the "God within" – remains a secret, a tremendous, fascinating, numinous mystery.   It is a "radioactive nucleus," to use Pauli's metaphor. And it has a timeless, holistic, trans-personal nature.

KS: What are our final conclusions concerning the connection between Jung and Taoism?   What do we finally learn about encountering the numinous within ourselves? What do we finally learn when we discover that each of us is much more than merely his or her own little individual ego?

WG: I'm not sure if there are any *final* conclusions, unless we conclude that we should continue to live the questions in order to evoke our ultimate concerns. Perhaps we need to look at Jung as something more than a great psychotherapist who broke away from his mentor Freud. Perhaps we need to look upon Jung as a great master of meditation, following in the succession of great masters since Lao-tze, and in his creative originality, eclipsing even such contemporaries as the Zen masters Suzuki and Dürckheim. We can especially see this through his experientially substantiated advocacy of the essence of meditation.

I'll return full circle by referring back to Jung's response to Ruth Topping, with which I began this part of the dialogue. There, he says that what is required is "concentrated attention, much mental work, and above all patience, the rarest thing in our restless and crazy time." It is this attentive patience which actually helps us to open ourselves to the numinous and thereby to transcend the nihilistic dangers within ourselves. This is the path of self-realization.

KS: It is clear from your connections drawn here that Jungian depth-psychology has its foundations in spirituality and that spirituality has an entirely personal as well as *trans-personal* basis.

WG: Yes. And as we have been suggesting, much the same is true of Taoism.   That philosophically religious or religiously philosophical outlook has long impressed me as being imbued with a kind of "natural grace." It reminds me of St. Thomas Aquinas's dialectic of nature as the "preface to grace" and grace as the "perfection" or completion of nature.[39]

KS: You think, then, that spirituality should also be thought of in terms of the Christian concept of Grace?

WG: Yes, I do! Grace is often defined as a free gift, an unmerited favor. I also like to think of Grace as a kind of "boundary crossing." Jung's psychology and Taoism teach us the importance of crossing boundaries in our everyday lives. Boundary crossing is a two-way street. The beauty of crossing boundaries is the *cross-fertilization process* that often takes place.

KS: The thought occurs to me that dialogue itself, from its archetypal philosophical expression in Plato to our infinitely more modest effort here, illustrates this very point.

WG: Indeed. One of my esteemed teachers, William Ernest Hocking, in his monumental *The Meaning of God in Human Experience*, saw this as the very essence of dynamic religion: cross-fertilization between and among world religions and cross-fertilization between work and worship in one's life. He called the latter the principle of alternation.

KS: What are some other specific examples of boundary-crossing?

WG: *Freely offered friendship*, to be sure. That is, something that is not just a one-shot deal, but capable of continuity. Closely related is *collegiality*, which is important in our professional lives. And then there is *marriage*. I do not mean marriage simply in the personal sense but also in a trans-personal, archetypal sense.

KS: And marriage is also symbolic of the "mutual arising" or "interdependent origination" that you have been emphasizing?

WG: Marriage is certainly one of the most powerful ways of presenting these ideas, which we have seen are so prominent in the thought of Jung and Lao-tze. And I have also come to think about marriage as a symbolic reality in three respects: (1) covenantal, (2) sacramental, and (3) transcendental.

KS: What do you mean, exactly?

WG: The covenantal dimension is expressed in the marriage vow: "To have and to hold, from this day forward, for better, for worse, for richer, for poorer, in sickness and in health, to love and to cherish, till death do us part, according to God's Holy Ordinance ..." That is the covenant. It is a publicly given vow. Now that covenant is also a sacrament. A sacrament – as I recall the Book of Common Prayer defines it – is "an outward and visible sign of an *inward and spiritual grace.*" I believe that there is a dimension of marriage that is internal. In addition to the outer public marriage, there is an *inner marriage* in which you identify with the other as an equal before God and with yourself.

KS: So we are speaking again of a dialectical coincidence of opposites, in the sense of a direct correlation between public or outer marriage and private or inner marriage.

WG: Yes. Just as the covenant of marriage will make out of our polarities and vicissitudes (of better-worse, richer-poorer, sickness-health) a unity of opposites and bring them to coincide. You know Jesus' famous statement, of course: "The kingdom of God is within you." This reminds us again of Jung's idea of "the God within" as the psychological center that unifies all opposites. That in itself, as profound as it seems, is symbolic of a third, or *transcendental*, dimension of marriage, the *heiros gamos*, from the Greek for "sacred marriage," as we have seen. And so the idea of a "transcendental" or "sacred" marriage presupposes the very idea that we have been emphasizing: self-realization as a type of *in-dividuation* or *making whole.*[40]

KS: And so we return, by way of the symbol of marriage, to our themes of self-realization, holism, synchronicity, and complementarity.

WG: Yes, full circle, if you will, like a mandala. Jung's idea of individuation involves a type of circularity, as we have seen: the re-integration of the ego with the Self. The archetype of the Self should also be viewed as the circumference as well as the center of the human psyche.

KS: Time can also be viewed in circular, rather than merely linear, terms. This might be a good way to review some of our findings. In our dialogue thus far we have mainly looked to the past while addressing a problem that confronts us today, that of nihilism. We discussed, in terms of both existential and psychological perspectives, the decline of older, institutional forms of religion and the emergence of a new and more open-ended spirituality. Nietzsche, Jung, Tillich, and Dürckheim were our guiding thinkers here, along with Hegel and Otto. We have also attempted to draw certain connections between the themes of that discussion – most especially Jung's ideas of individuation, synchronicity, and the timeless as well as trans-personal nature of the Self – and the broad currents of Taoism. Jung and Dürckheim have provided us with a nice transition between East and West, if you will.

WG: I agree. Now it would be timely to consider the future prospects of Jung's psychology.

KS: Let's do it then.

EPILOGUE

THE FUTURE OF JUNG'S PSYCHOLOGY

Kevin Stoehr: Bill, as you have suggested, our previous dialogue has connected Jungian depth-psychology with the problem of nihilism, the existential philosophy of Nietzsche, the systematic theology of Tillich, the meditative discipline of self-transformation in the thinking of Dürckheim, and the overall worldview of Taoism. The close links between Jung's thought and the deeper dimensions of human spirituality have become clearer. But more specifically, what does the future of Jung's psychology hold in store for us?

William Geoghegan: Good question! Let me respond in a roundabout sort of way. Recently I gave a talk to the Bowdoin College Jung Seminar, when I substituted for a previously-scheduled speaker who was unable to keep her commitment.[1] I had done a considerable amount of reading in which I was vitally interested the previous summer.

KS: Such as?

WG: Number one was James H. Austin's *Zen And The Brain: Toward an Understanding of Meditation and Consciousness*[2], which I shall emphasize later, and *Atom And Archetype: The Pauli-Jung Letters 1932-1958*, which I shall talk about more briefly.[3] These two books have helped to substantiate a growing awareness of what I take to be the primary thrust of Jung's psychology in the study of world philosophies and religions, especially as I anticipate how it may develop in the future.

I decided on a title, "The Future of Jung's Psychology," and began drafting my talk. Imagine my pleasant surprise when I learned in September from the Brunswick Jung Center Fall Newsletter that Anthony Stevens, MD, a distinguished London analyst and scholar who had delivered the inaugural Mildred E. Harris Annual Lecture in 1988, was to give a second Harris lecture, this one entitled "Archetypes, Jung's Psychology And The Future," on the Friday preceding my own talk.

KS: Synchronicity!

WG: Yes. A very good example. Moreover, Stevens's emphasis was on the *scientific* foundations of Jung's basic concept of the archetypes of the collective, or universal, unconscious, which he described as innate behavioral and psychological propensities manifested in the evolutionary history of the human species.[4]   This close link between analytical psychology and evolutionary biology re-inforced my own growing interest in exploring the relations between Jung's psychology and neuroscience and quantum theory.

KS: This is quite a shift of perspective, isn't it?

WG: To be sure. But ultimately it gets us back to the main point. Before moving on, however, I want to glance back to the Spring of 2001 when Bowdoin College's Department of Religion sponsored a conference featuring four notable religion scholars on "The Future of the Academic Study of Religion." A colleague who over-heard me saying that I was on my way to the conference asked "Does *religion* have a *future*?" My instant unthinking (i.e., unconscious) response was, "Religion *is* the future." For over a half-century my professional life has been devoted to the study and teaching of world religions, especially their philosophical dimension, as embodying and reflecting innate or archetypal propensities of humanity.

KS: Yes, as in Otto's concept of the numinous, awesome mystery, simultaneously disturbing and magnetizing.

WG: Exactly. And my point is that the events of September 11, 2001 – especially the spectacle of the crashing of the two hi-jacked planes into the twin towers of the World Trade Center in lower Manhattan – have formed a striking contemporary archetypal *image* (*Bild*) of the truly awesome in its stunning impact and fathomless implications. After this epochal event one wonders whether the question of religion's future will seriously be asked again.

KS: Because religion's essence is timeless.

WG: That's right. Further, I recently became acquainted with the major thesis of Samuel P. Huntington, a University Professor at Harvard, who contends in a recent book that all extant civilizations – the three major ones being Western, Islamic and Chinese – are substantively defined by their religions and that in the new multi-polar world order the "Clash of Civilizations" will be at bottom a clash of religions.[5]

KS: *Jihads?*

WG: His many critics seem to think so – and in the most obvious sense of the word *jihad*. But as you may know, in the primary meaning of the word in the *Koran*, it means a moral and spiritual "struggle" and "effort."[6]

KS: And we can view Jung as a fruitful source of insight in that primary spiritual sense?

WG: Exactly. But more specifically, I believe it is time for Jung's psychology to undergo a "de-pathologization" as being *primarily* a form of psychotherapy. This rather narrow view of Jung's thought has led to its subsequent "ghetto-ization," forcing it outside of the main currents of contemporary thought. In Pauli's phrase, Jung's thought is more like a "religious philosophical system" or wisdom teaching than anything else. In my way of thinking, Jung's thought, more specifically, should be considered as *a spiritual exercise or practice and way of life*. As such, it would be more akin to worldviews with a numinous charge – as in Buddhism, Stoicism, and the mysticism of a Meister Eckhart or a Shankara – than a time-bound species of Western psychotherapy. Moreover, as a spiritual practice it would also take its place in the spectrum of developing scientific theory and research.

KS: I know you've always had great respect for science, but isn't this something new?

WG: Yes, in a sense it is, but my thesis reflects not only a long interest in philosophy of religion but also some pertinent recent experience from the burgeoning field of mind/body medicine.

KS: Tell me about this experience.

WG: Since 1995 I have attended three Harvard Medical School Continuing Education courses on mind/body medicine, courses which I have interpreted as a barometer of the relevance of Jung's psychology to that field.

KS: How so?

WG: Well, in the first two courses, "Spirituality and Healing in Medicine" (1995) and the same "with Emphasis on Death and Dying" (1998), Jung was cited only once, but quite significantly:

> I should like to call attention to the following facts. During the past thirty years, people from all the civilized countries of the earth have consulted me. Many hundreds of patients have passed through my hands, the greater number being Protestants, a lesser number Jews, and not more than five or six believing Catholics. Among all my patients in the second half of life – that is to say, over thirty-five – there has not been one whose problem in the last resort was not that of finding a religious outlook on life. It is safe to say that every one of them fell ill because he had lost what the living religions of every age have given to their followers, and none of them has been really healed who did not regain his religious outlook.[7]

KS: We have touched upon this before, have we not?

WG: Indeed we have. But I think the point is worth emphasizing, especially in the context of the third course, "Science and Mind/Body Medicine" (May 2001), which in my view marked a new and major departure for the role of Jung's psychology.

KS: In what way?

WG: One of the great 20th century pioneers in the development of mind/body medicine, Herbert Benson, a Professor of Medicine at Harvard Medical School and the author of the ground-breaking "The Relaxation Response," among other similar works, had been sole Director in all previous courses.

KS: I remember your great respect for Dr. Benson.

WG: Yes. On this occasion he was joined by a Co-Director, who was also given top billing. This was Richard L. Kradin, M.D., an Associate Professor at Harvard Medical School and Director of Research at the

Mind/Body Institute. Significantly, at the same time, Dr. Kradin was an analyst-in-training at the Jung Institute in Boston.

KS: In our context, that is indeed significant.

WG: Additionally, I attended a major presentation, "Dreams and Health," made by a Jungian analyst, in this case Robert Bosnak, J.D., who practices in Boston and Japan. And Dr. Kradin himself gave two major presentations, the first on "Neuroscience Interactions" and the second on "The Scientific Basis of the Religious Psyche." In addition, in his introductions to the lectures and in his moderation of the question periods following, he highlighted the connections among such varied and relevant topics as chaos theory, mental mapping, and nervous system pathways.

KS: Interesting. But I don't quite see yet the connection with Jung's psychology.

WG: Right. I'm coming to that, but first let me point out that much of the foregoing and what followed was connected and placed in historical context by the first scheduled speaker, Eugene Taylor, Ph.D., a lecturer in psychiatry at Harvard Medical School, and a major William James scholar. His talk on the history of mind/body medicine paralleled in many respects his recent book *Shadow Culture: Psychology and Spirituality in America.*[8] In this book he describes three religious "Great Awakenings," or major waves of renewal in American religious history, each accompanied by a "shadow," or a non-mainstream, non-establishment, "visionary tradition." The first wave was in the colonial period, the second a few decades before the Civil War, and the third originated in the 1960's and continues in the proliferation of multitudinous varieties of spirituality, including Jung's psychology.

KS: How did Jung come to play a role in this "third wave"?

WG: For example, as Taylor emphasizes in Chapter 10, "The Americanization of Jung and Freud," the priority given to Jung in the title is noteworthy. He presents the evidence that, for the first part of the 20th century, Jung's psychology was better known than Freud's among psychiatric professionals in America. This was because of the close and frequent contact between leading members of the American psychiatric establishment, centered in Boston, and the Swiss establishment centered at the Burghölzli, the mental hospital of the University of Zürich. There Jung was a lecturer and first assistant to its director, Eugen Bleuler.

KS: Eugen Bleuler. I seem to recall from Ellenberger's book that Bleuler coined the term "schizophrenia".

WG: Correct! But to proceed: Jung had also become well-known in Europe and America for his empirical studies in the word-association test (which, incidentally, was the basis for his initial and fateful contact with Freud).

KS: Speaking of Freud, how did Jung's one-time mentor fare in the discussion of the role of spirituality and healing in medicine?

WG: Good question. His dismissal of religion as a "universal obsessional neurosis" and of religious philosophy and the like as "the black tide of mud of the occult" resulted, after brief mention, in his own dismissal.

KS: That's not surprising. Do you think that this by-passing of Freud might also reflect the considerable diminishing of his prominence in America since the sixties, while Jung's influence has grown, especially in connection with the efflorescence of so many forms of spirituality?

WG: I think so. Moreover, the growing influence of Jung's psychology in mind/body medicine, as witnessed by Taylor, Bosnak, and Kradin, serves as an introduction to the role of Jung's psychology in the work of James H. Austin, M.D., who lectured on his *magnum opus, Zen and the Brain.*

KS: Tell me more about him.

WG: He is Professor Emeritus of Neurology at the University of Colorado Health Science Center, Affiliate Professor of Philosophy at the University of Idaho, and a life-long adult practitioner of Zen Buddhism. His *Zen And The Brain* is an encyclopedic treatise, weighing in at 5 pounds, numbering some 850 pages, and consisting of three major distinct yet extensively inter-related parts.

Approximately one-third of Austin's work is a neuroscience text-book on the physiology and biochemistry of the triune human brain, a subject in which I have had no previous training, but which I struggled with nevertheless. Another third is a detailed scholarly treatise on the history, philosophy, and practice of Zen Buddhism, featuring Master Dogen. The final third consists of wide-ranging historical, philosophical, psychological and personal reflections on spirituality and mysticism, virtually equating these latter two terms.

KS: Bill, I can sympathize with your struggle with neuroscience, but I can see why you did it because of your long-standing interest in the other two parts. However, I do have one question: You say that Austin virtually equates "spirituality and mysticism." What do you think of that claim? Is it valid?

WG: The short answer is, Yes. And I'll amplify this as we proceed. Meanwhile, I want to focus on the main point, which is Austin's use of Jung's psychology in corroborating his own position on spirituality and mysticism at the *psychological* level.

KS: But, tell me, what do you see as the main point Austin is trying to make that is relevant to that psychological level?

WG: As I read it, the gist of the book is an argument that Zen meditation, above all its "peak experience" of *satori* (or *kensho*, as Austin prefers), transforms the physiology and biochemistry of the brain and consequently the rest of the body and its associated mind, soul, and spirit.

KS: And this fits in with Jung's concept of individuation as the process of coming to recognize one's inherent undividedness or wholeness.

WG: Indeed. Moreover, Austin boldly sets his entire three-fold discussion in the context of what he calls "mysticism in the most general sense," defined as "the ongoing practice of re-establishing, by the deepest insights, one's direct relationship with the ultimate, universal reality principle."[9] Note how, in this excellent generic definition of mysticism, each term or phrase counts, both singularly and also, as we shall see, in terms of our subsequent exposition of its relation to Jung's psychology. For example:

> (1)   "on-going practice" clearly implies something not speculative, but active, a doing;
>
> (2)   "re-establishing" implies a practice as something that

is not novel or "creative," but as a *ressourcement*;

(3)   "by the deepest insights" is a phrase referring to that which is intuitively self-evident;

(4)   "one's direct relationship" implies an immediate union with the "ultimate, universal reality principle."

KS: There is certainly nothing trivial about these claims.

WG: Nothing trivial. That's why I find them truly interesting. They speak for themselves. Nevertheless, it is worth noting that the "ultimate, universal reality principle" *independently* reflects the basic perspective on the spiritual core or essence of religion in the thought of the 20th century's best-known American historian of world religions, Huston Smith. He emphasizes this perspective in his major work *The World's Religions.*[10] And for Rudolph Otto the pre-eminent manifestation of the essence of religion as the numinous is its mystical element.[11] This general concept of mysticism, considered as the core of "spirituality" itself as well as the essence of the perennial philosophy or primordial tradition is, as we have noted, congruent with Jung's basic concept of individuation.

KS: How would you spell that out at this point and in this connection?

WG: Well, for Jung, as we have seen, "individuation" refers to the dynamic equilibrium between the ego, the center of conscious identity, and the Self (German: *das Selbst*), experienced as the inner and outer "collective (or universal) unconscious" – i.e., the unknown which, while completely transcending the ego, is paradoxically not unrelated to it.[12] While it is clear that Jung's concept of individuation – becoming one whole – is primarily *psychological*, it is also *philosophical* in the tradition of Socrates and Plato.

KS: You are thinking here once again of the Socratic emphasis that "the unexamined life is not worth living" and that "the care of the self" or "tendance of the soul" is the paramount life-task.[13]

WG: Absolutely. It is a key point, if not *the* key point! Moreover, even from the ultimate monistic mystical perspective of Zen that Jung does not share as such, Austin finds a number of Jung's basic concepts to be psychologically and philosophically useful. For example, Jung's concept of the "collective unconscious" is fundamental for Austin as, for example, when he quotes Jung's striking formulation: "We must get at the Eastern values from within and not from without, seeking them in ourselves in the unconscious. We shall then discover how great is our fear of the unconscious and how formidable are our resistances."[14]

KS: Yes, that is striking. Would you say that the distinctiveness lies in the combining of a classical introspective or introvertive mysticism with the analytical insights of 20th century depth-psychology?

WG: I would, but I would also point out that while for Jung the ultimate goal is individuation, for Austin it is *kensho* as reflected in his general definition of mysticism. In contrast to Jung, for whom the ego in the individuation process is *transformed*, for Austin it is *dissolved*. And like all authentic mystical experiences, *kensho* is ultimately ineffable. The closest that Austin comes to describing what *kensho* is *like*, as distinct from the actual experience, is "the peace that passeth all understanding."[15]

KS: Do you think that Jung would agree with Austin about the ineffability of the ultimate state of consciousness, best expressed as "the peace that passeth all understanding"?

WG: I do.

KS: So despite certain over-arching agreements between Austin and Jung in terms of their emphasis upon the "universal reality principle" and our relation to it, there is a definite contrast between Jungian individuation and the Zen state of *kensho*, especially in terms of how they view the ultimate status of the human ego?

WG: Yes, but there are also other close connections to be drawn here that soften the contrast. Moving back, so to speak, to the lower stage of consciousness closest to *kensho*, we find an extraordinary congruence between *intuition* – one of Jung's four basic psychological functions –and *prajna*, or "insight-wisdom," as Austin brilliantly translates the Sanskrit term for the way of knowing that transcends all lower stages of consciousness. For example, in support of his view of *prajna*, Austin cites the following from Jung:

> Certain contents issue from a psyche that is more complete than consciousness. They often contain a superior analysis or insight or

knowledge which consciousness has not been able to produce. We have a suitable word for such occurrences – intuition.[16]

KS: That is putting an awful lot of weight on a word that is often very casually used.

WG: True. Nevertheless both Austin and Jung are speaking directly from their own experience that it is by means of direct insight and in no other way that we truly know "the ultimate, universal reality principle."

Austin also uses examples from Jung's life and thought to draw parallels between individuation and the arduous *Zazen* process of attaining insight-wisdom and ineffable peace. First of all, he begins Chapter 140, "Preludes with Potential: Dark Nights and Depressions," with the following from Jung: "The steep path of self-development is ... as mournful and gloomy as the path to Hell."[17]

KS: That does sound grim.

WG: It *is* grim, but in a most profound sense. We are talking here about "ultimate concern." This rather Nietzschean theme of the productive uses of adversity was basic to Austin's initial Zen meditation experience. He speaks movingly of the "unbearable torture" of the pains in his knees and thighs, dryly adding that he was told by his *roshi*, Dr. Osumi, that "Zazen is good for the central nervous sytem, but bad for the peripheral nervous system."[18]

KS: That sounds a bit like gallows humor to me.

WG: It does. But continuing to pursue the link between neurology and mystical spirituality, Austin analyzes the objectivity of the visions experienced by Jung during his near-fatal heart attack in 1944 at the age of 69.[19] In this classic near-death experience, Jung was convinced of the objective reality of his visions of the Cabbalistic and Christian *hieros gamos* (sacred marriage) and its analogous alchemical *mysterium coniunctionis*. Jung writes:

> I would never have imagined that any such experience was possible. It was not a product of imagination. The visions and experiences were utterly real; there was nothing subjective about them; they all had a quality of absolute objectivity.[20]

KS: I take it that Austin accepts this report at face value.

WG: It would appear so, since he goes on to add that Jung had a similar vision of his wife after her death. For Jung these visions testified to the ultimate point attained in his process of individuation. As he wrote, this *coniunctio* with oneself is marked by the withdrawal of emotional projections and "an unconditional 'Yes' to that which is."[21]

KS: With this mention of "an unconditional 'Yes" to that which is," I think here again of Nietzsche's principles of *Amor fati* and eternal recurrence, along with your mention a moment ago of the productive uses of adversity as a theme in Jung and Austin. Wouldn't this "unconditional 'Yes'" be in complete accord with many similar experientially-based statements from mystics and sages, East and West, past and present?

WG: I believe so, but I would like to make the observation that on the way to *prajna* and *kensho* – insight-wisdom and ineffable peace – there are also near-term stages of consciousness which are of great practical importance. While these may be described in Jungian terms as a de-flating or de-centering the ego, as a neurologist Austin confidently affirms that all egos are *constructs of our brains* during the first eighteen months of infant life.

KS: What an astonishing claim! Austin holds that our "I's," what we think of as our very selves, are *fictions*? Do you think then that Austin is a "reductionist"?

WG: On the contrary, so far as consciousness is concerned I would call him an "expansionist." These constructs develop into the deeply rooted, commonplace, existential orientation of "I-ME-MINE." Consequently, the purpose of *Zazen* is to dissolve this "selfish" ego and cultivate a "pragmatic" one. In the course of this process, the original upper case "I-ME-MINE" ego-orientation, as he puts it, is gradually transformed into a lower case "i-me-mine" one, marked by the "on-going positive traits" of being "**A**ctualized, **B**ouyant, **C**ompassionate" – the ABC's of Zen.[22]

KS: This seems a bit simplistic, if I may say.

WG: Perhaps. But remember, he is addressing middle-range, transitional states of consciousness on the way to the ultimate *prajna-kensho* state. Austin writes:

> [t]he brain's intuitive capacities reach their peak. At impact, a totally unifying objective vision comprehends the whole outside world, just as it really is. It registers as immanent eternal perfection. Fear vanishes because the entire I-ME-MINE drops out at every affective level.[23]

KS: A breathtaking claim.

WG: And note how it tallies with the quite similar experience he cited from Jung. Moreover, even with his ultimate monistic perspective, Austin is not oblivious to what Jung called "the problem of opposites." As he points out in his chapter on "Aging in the Brain," following Jung, after the age of 35 the "zig-zag" process of self-development or self-realization has as its goal "the reconciliation of opposites."[24] That is, in the second half of life we begin to realize the value of the opposites of our former ideals and, in this process of self-realization, energy previously consumed in the struggle between opposites now vitalizes the uniting of ego and Self.[25]

KS: This process of reversal seems to be another good example of the "enantiodromia" or "running contrariwise" to which Jung frequently refers.[26]

WG: Yes. Further, for Austin, the "ripening" and "pruning" process in the aging brain facilitates the transformation of "I-ME-MINE" into "WE-YOU-OURS." This occurs through what William James called elders' skill in "artful over-looking," along with the emergence of a "mellow wisdom" and its "big picture" perspective.[27]

KS: And so the future of Jungian thought, taking Austin's book as our lead, takes the shape of a broad convergence among current fields such as depth-psychology, spirituality, comparative religion, neuroscience, and mind-body medicine generally.

WG: Yes. That seems clear – and promising – to me. Further, in the light of Austin's use of Jung's psychology in clarifying the meaning of Zen Buddhism, one can reasonably expect other neuroscience researchers who focus on spirituality and mystical religion also to find material of great value in Jung's psychology (always making allowance for necessary differences, as in the case of the final status of the ego in Jung and Austin). Austin is a learned and broad-minded neuroscientist and a dedicated and enthusiastic Zen advocate. At the same time, his presentation of Zen is well within the central mystical thrust of world religions, as witnessed by his generic definition of mysticism. He acknowledges that neuroscience is in its infancy and he recognizes the inherent limitations of scientific method at its most basic level. He shares with quantum physicist Max Planck the view that "in the last analysis we ourselves are part of nature, and therefore part of the mystery we are trying to solve."[28] One is reminded of St. Augustine's famous self-realization: "I became a mystery to myself."

KS: How about the future of Jungian thought in terms of *philosophy*?

WG: Well, as you know, I think of *philosophy* primarily in the Socratic sense – in terms of philosophical and personal *dialogue* and in terms of seeking self-knowledge.

KS: Living the questions!

WG: Exactly. And in pursuing our theme of the relation of Jung's psychology to science at the philosophical level, we might consider the dialogue between Jung and quantum physicist Wolfgang Pauli.

KS: Yes, and this returns us once again to the convergence between Jungian thought, spirituality, and 20th century science. Please say more about this convergence, Bill.

WG: Well, Jung and Pauli had their first contact in 1932 when they began an exchange of nearly one hundred letters over a period of 26 years. Although Pauli stood at the top of his profession, the peer of his close friend and colleague Niels Bohr, he had a troubled personality and a background of a dysfunctional family of origin, alcohol abuse, and disturbing dreams. He sought medical attention from Jung.

KS: So Jung analyzed Pauli?

WG: No. Curiously, he did not. Instead he delegated the task to an associate so that he might interpret Pauli's dreams as objectively as possible.[29] Altogether he reviewed some 1300 of Pauli's dreams and selected about 400 for use on his *Psychology and Alchemy and The Analysis of Dreams*.[30] Significantly, in my view, they collaborated on the subject of "Synchronicity" in "The Interpretation of Nature and Psyche."[31]

KS: So their dialogue was unusual in that it consisted of dream interpretation, correspondence, occasional interviews, and scholarly collaboration, rather than through face-to-face conversation?

WG: Yes. But it was nonetheless a robust *philosophical and spiritual dialogue,* in which each influenced the other in his thinking at the most fundamental ontological level. For Pauli, however, in accord with Jung, the essential spiritual problem was not (as with Austin) the existence of the ego *per se* but rather the "problem of opposites" – especially the *split* between Psyche (soul, mind) and Physis (Nature).

KS: Both Jung and Pauli, it would appear, share a common view of how to address this "problem of opposites."

WG: Exactly. And they both address this problem through the imaginal language of alchemy and Gnosticism.[32] Thus the principles of *unus mundus* (One World) and the *hieros gamos* (sacred marriage) respectively symbolize the ultimate union striven for by transcendental spiritual love, also associated by Jung with the archetypal feminine, the "anima."[33]

KS: And they share these ideas on more-or-less equal terms?

WG: It would appear so. For both, alchemy was a projection into the physical world of the transformation of psychological "lead" into spiritual "gold" and of a split universe into a holistic one.

KS: Hegel's "The truth is the whole ..."

WG: Yes! In addition, moving beyond Jung, Pauli devoted special attention to Johannes Kepler, the early 17th century mathematician and astronomer who also practiced alchemy. Pauli portrays Kepler as a major transitional figure, bridging the gap between high scientific achievement (as in his Three Laws of Planetary Motion) and timeless striving toward the ideal of the *unus mundus*. Additionally, however, as might be expected, Pauli also emphasized, much more than Jung, the physical side of the cosmic and symbolic significance of alchemy. Thus, he concludes, all of nature is an "abstract dance of particles" governed by the quantum principles of "symmetry" and "exclusion," such that each particle is profoundly influenced by the Whole.[34]

KS: That's a fascinating conclusion. Is there anything else that you would like to say about the Jung-Pauli dialogue?

WG: Yes, Kevin, I'd like to touch upon a few more ideas. In a letter to Aniela Jaffé, Jung's devoted amanuensis and biographer, Pauli wrote that there were only two fundamental and non-contradictory "religious philosophical systems": (1) the static or cyclical system, as in Taoism (which he greatly respected, yet regretfully put aside) and (2) the "evolutionary," or dynamic, system, as in Jung's psychology, conceived as the human response to the unbounded "radioactive nucleus" of the archetype of the Self as "God-image." The latter was the system which Pauli preferred.[35]

KS: That image of the Self as a "radioactive nucleus" is stunning.

WG: I should say so. The context suggests that Jung himself was somewhat taken aback by it. At the very least, it is a thought-provoking image. I wish we had time to go into it in more detail.

KS: At least let me try to summarize the state of the question. We have examined themes and traces of these two fundamental systems (or *dialectical poles*) via Jungian lenses throughout our earlier conversation. Their compatibility, as we seem to agree, referring to the life and work of Jung, is problematic but not impossible. They suggest two distinct yet seemingly interrelated modes of personal relationship to Mystery and the Unconscious.

WG: Yes. Let me offer a contemporary illustration of the kind of thing we are dealing with here. Following the tradition of quantum speculation from Pauli to the present, it is worth noting some recent comments by the esteemed physicist John A. Wheeler, who was recently honored at a symposium at Princeton University on "Science and Ultimate Reality." After a year in the early 1930's in Copenhagen with Niels Bohr, Wheeler is reported to have said later, "You can talk about people like Buddha, Jesus, Moses, Confucius, but the thing that convinced me that such people existed were conversations with Bohr." In expounding his view, shared by other quantum physicists, that in the final analysis the universe is created by human observation, Wheeler (in a journal notation of January 29, 2002) wrote: "No space, no time, no gravity, no electro-magnetism, no particles. Nothing. We are back where Plato, Aristotle and Parmenides struggled with the great questions: How come the Universe? How come us? How come anything? But happily also we have the answer to these questions. That's us." [36]

KS: And so quantum physics returns us to the fundamental questions of existence, the questions once posed by the great metaphysical and ontological thinkers.

WG: Absolutely. However, one may agree whole-heartedly with Wheeler about the genius of Bohr and the importance of the questions of Plato, Aristotle, and Parmenides (not to mention Heraclitus and myriad successors) without the immodest supposition that we are the "answer." I don't believe that genuine philosophy or science or theology or religion has anything to do with that kind of presumptuous "closure."

KS: Nevertheless, we have found some general connections among the ideas of scientific thinkers such as Pauli, Wheeler, and Austin, on the one hand, and the ideas of philosophical or spiritual thinkers who range from Lao-tze to Rudolf Otto and Huston Smith, on the other hand. Jung seems to rest at the center of this web, in many ways.

WG: Yes. Or to change the metaphor, Jung's psychology resides in a kind of "quantum state" between the poles you mention.

KS: Could you be more explicit?

WG: I'll try. I think that Jung, Austin and Pauli, taken together, provide a wonderfully fresh and exciting discussion of the human individual's "direct relationship" with the "universal reality principle." [37] Each – psychologist, neurologist, and physicist – conceives the essential meaning of human existence as a *nisus*, "a mental or physical effort to attain an end: a perfective urge or endeavor," in this case toward an ultimate unity, the whole. [38] Taken together, the likes of Jung, Austin, and Pauli might also well serve as a wake-up call to those who wish to repose undisturbed in their "dogmatic slumbers," to steal a phrase from Immanuel Kant. [39]

KS: I've always loved that phrase, "dogmatic slumbers." It's the complete antithesis to Rilke's "living the questions."

WG: It is indeed. And note also that while all three are ultimately holistic in their fundamental intellectual and spiritual orientations, Austin, with his experience of *kensho*, is the closest of these thinkers to the absolute unity which excludes all dualism, even that between good and evil. In contrast to Austin, Jung and Pauli wrestle strenuously with the "problem of evil." They squarely face the contradiction between the ultimate vision of irreducible unity, on the one hand, and the experiential reality of intractable evil, on the other. Pauli expresses great admiration for Jung's agonized *Answer to Job* and shares his emphatic rejection of the traditional Plotinian-Augustinian doctrine of evil as not a reality in itself, but as a privation or absence of the good (*privatio boni*). Along with the emotional turmoil of his life, Pauli was quite sensitive to what he regarded as moral evil. For example, although he had many opportunities to do so, he refused to participate in the Manhattan Project for reasons of conscience.[40]

KS: And yet, Bill, in spite of these differences, Austin is not alone in his insistence upon an ultimate and absolute metaphysical unity. Its experiential and theoretical reality is testified to in many philosophical and religious traditions, and especially in Asian and Western antiquity, as we have seen.

WG: I couldn't agree more. For the time being, perhaps, it would be best to allow *this* "problem of opposites" to play itself out, in the light of Bohr's famous assertion that "the opposite of a true statement is a false statement, but the opposite of a profound truth may be another profound truth." [41]

KS: Yes, I can see more clearly what John Wheeler meant when he ranked Bohr right up there with those iconic figures in philosophy and religion.

WG: And, in addition, in the moving conclusion to his "Late Thoughts," where Jung pays tribute to the supreme value of "cosmogonic love," as in *I Corinthians* 13, he confesses that even to call the idea of absolute unity "God" is to "name the unknown by the more unknown." (By the way, Jung is not alone in this view, which has a distinguished heritage in the philosophical tradition.[42]) I sometimes visualize Jung in his later years, after the death of his wife Emma, as he retreated more and more into his sanctuary at Bollingen, in the primordial silence and darkness musing upon the proverbial *Secretum meum mihi*: "My secret is my own."

KS: But if, as you seem to see Jung suggesting, that all ends in mystery, what is there left to say?

WG: While we should defer any claim to a non-experiential resolution of the ultimate metaphysical question of absolute unity, as we must, we may continue to look nevertheless toward the near-term future of Jung's psychology.

KS: How so?

WG: I believe, to repeat what I stated at the beginning, that it lies in three areas, taken together: (1) mind-body or integrative medicine in general, and neuroscience specifically, for example, as shown in Austin's work; (2) in vigorous and original philosophical dialogue, as illustrated in the Pauli-Jung correspondence; and (3) in a transformative spirituality, as implied in Jung's notion of "cosmogonic love" and Pauli's image of the Self as a "radioactive nucleus." In this light, Jung's psychology should be regarded not as a fixed doctrine, or *primarily* a psycho-therapy, but as a *spiritual practice or exercise* defined as "an activity that requires spiritual and mental exertion, especially when intended to develop or maintain spiritual growth." [43]

KS: In many ways, it would seem that this notion of a *spiritual practice or exercise* applies even to an atheistic philosopher such as Nietzsche.

WG: Yes. Paradoxically, especially to Nietzsche, as we have observed. We have also seen earlier in our conversation how Nietzsche's philosophy, and especially *Thus Spake Zarathustra*, was creatively interpreted by Jung as a spiritual practice. And as we have also seen, Jung identifies the turning-point in Nietzsche's spiritual journey or *Geistesodyssey* in *Zarathustra* as that in which he exclaims "There one became two and Zarathustra passed me by." This statement clearly expresses the visionary living nature of the Zarathustra experience.[44]

KS: As you pointed out earlier, Jung sees Nietzsche's encounter with

Zarathustra as comparable to his own initiatory experience in which analytical psychology originated.

WG: Quite right. And if you recall, I mentioned the three German verbs that the French analyst Elie Humbert emphasizes in discussing the spiritual dimension of Jung's method of "active imagination": *Geschehenlassen* or "letting happen," *Betrachten* or "contemplation," and *Sich auseinandersetzen* or "confrontation."[45] I would like to call attention to these verbs once again, as they are quite helpful in substantiating the view that Jung's thought, like Nietzsche's, is rooted in a profoundly spiritual quality of experience. Such an experience is the departure point for spiritual exercise and the source of Jung's, as well as Nietzsche's, works and creativity.

KS: In a sense, these verbs express the central turning-point of Jung's life, his transformative spiritual experience.

WG: This seems undoubtedly the case. Moreover, we have also already recognized the important parallel in the work of Meister Eckhart, with his *Gelazenheit* (releasement), *Abgeschiedenheit* (detachment), and *Durchbruch* (breakthrough). This parallel points to the essential *spiritual* foundation of Jung's psychology.

Thus, from its creative origins, Jung's psychology matured into a spiritual practice and way of life. In the final analysis it should be considered as an exemplary wisdom teaching and we might well view Jung himself, in spite of his not infrequently noted human failings, as a sage, similar in many respects to those found in various world philosophies, religions, and wisdom traditions.

KS: With that, Bill, we really seem to have come full circle.

WG: Yes. We have now returned to our starting-point – Jung's psychology as a spiritual practice and a way of life.

KS: And "living the questions" sums it up, Bill.

WG: Yes, Kevin. Living the questions sums it up.

END NOTES

Introduction: Ultimate Concern

1. For example, Tillich tells us: "There are innumerable concerns in our lives and in human life generally which demand attention, devotion, passion. But they do not demand *infinite* attention, *unconditional* devotion, *ultimate* passion. They are important, often very important for you and for me and for the whole of mankind. But they are not *ultimately* important." (Paul Tillich, "Our Ultimate Concern," excerpted from Tillich's *The New Being*, appearing in *The Essential Tillich: An Anthology of the Writings of Paul Tillich*, ed. F. Forrester Church [NY: Macmillan Publishing Company, 1987], p. 33.)
2. William D. Geoghegan, *Platonism in Recent Religious Thought* (New York: Columbia University Press, 1958).

Part One: The Essence of Spiritedness and the Emergence of a New Spirituality

1. Rainer Maria Rilke, *Letters to a Young Poet* (1903), transl. Stephen Mitchell (NY: Random House, 1984), pp. 34-5.
2. See Paul Tillich, *The Courage To Be*, Second Edition, with an Introduction by Peter J. Gomes (New Haven and London: Yale University Press, 2000), pp. xi-xxxiii. Quoted comment can be found on the back cover of this edition.
3. C. G. Jung, *Memories, Dreams, Reflections*, ed. Aniela Jaffé, transl. Richard and Clara Winston, Revised Edition (NY: Vintage Books, A Division of Random House, 1965), p. 3.
4. Jung: "For me the world has from the beginning been infinite and ungraspable." (Ibid., p. 356) "There is nothing I am quite sure about. I have no definite convictions – not about anything, really. I know only that I was born and exist, and it seems to me that I have been carried along. I exist on the foundation of something I do not know. In spite of all uncertainties, I feel a solidity underlying all existence and a continuity in my mode of being." (Ibid., p. 358)
5. As H. G. Baynes tells us in his essay "The Provisional Life": "(The provisional life) denotes an attitude that is innocent of responsibility toward the circumstantial facts of reality as though these facts are being provided for, either by the parents, or the state, or at least by Providence ... (It is) a state of childish irresponsibility and dependence." (Baynes, *Analytical Psychology and the English Mind* [London: Methuen and Co., Ltd., 1950], p. 61.)

6. Jung: "I have frequently seen people become neurotic when they content themselves with inadequate or wrong answers to the questions of life. They seek position, marriage, reputation, outward success or money, and remain unhappy and neurotic even when they have attained what they were seeking. Such people are usually confined within too narrow a spiritual horizon. Their life has not sufficient content, sufficient meaning. If they are enabled to develop into more spacious personalities, the neurosis generally disappears. For that reason the idea of development was always of the highest importance to me." (*Memories, Dreams, Reflections*, op. cit., p. 140)

7. Maurice Merleau-Ponty, *Sense and Non-sense* (Northwestern University Press, 1964), p. 63. Quoted in a footnote in Charles Taylor's *Hegel* (Cambridge: Cambridge University Press, 1991), p. 538.

8. Hegel: "The truth is the whole. The whole, however, is merely the essential nature reaching its completeness through the process of its own development." (G. W. F. Hegel, *The Phenomenology of Mind*, transl. J. B. Baillie [NY: Harper Torchbooks, Harper and Row, 1967], p. 81).

9. William Butler Yeats, "The Second Coming," from *Selected Poems and Two Plays of William Butler Yeats*, ed. M. L. Rosenthal (NY: Collier Books, The Macmillan Company, 1962), p. 91.

10. Tillich: "Protestantism is understood as a special historical embodiment of a universally significant principle. This principle, in which one side of the divine-human relationship is expressed, is effective in all periods of history ... There is no question here as to whether we are now approaching the end of the Protestant principle. This principle is not a special religious or cultural idea; it is not subject to the changes of history, it is not dependent on the increase or decrease of religious experience or spiritual power. It is the ultimate criterion of all religious and all spiritual experiences; it lies at their base, whether they are aware of it or not." (Paul Tillich, from *The Protestant Era* [Chicago: University of Chicago Press, 1957], xi-xxix. Also quoted in *The Essential Tillich*, ed. F. Forrester Church [NY: Macmillan Publishing Company, 1987], p. 69).

11. Tillich: "The state of existence is the state of estrangement. Man is estranged from the ground of his being, from other beings, and from himself. The transition from essence to existence results in personal guilt and universal tragedy ..." (Paul Tillich, from *Systematic Theology, Vol. II: Existence and the Christ* [Chicago: University of Chicago Press, 1957], pp. 44-47. Also quoted in *The Essential Tillich*, op. cit., p. 165).

12. See the chapter "On Redemption" in the Second Part of Nietzsche's *Thus Spoke Zarathustra*.

13. "At this point the real answer to the question, *how one becomes what one is*, can no longer be avoided. And thus I touch on the masterpiece of the art of self-preservation – of *selfishness*. For let us assume that the task, the destiny, the fate of the task transcends the average very significantly:

in that case, nothing could be more dangerous than catching sight of oneself *with* this task. To become what one is, one must not have the faintest notion *what* one is." (Nietzsche, "Why I Am So Clever," *Ecce Homo*, transl. and ed. Walter Kaufmann, appearing in *On the Genealogy of Morals and Ecce Homo* [NY: Vintage Books, Random House], 1989).

14. Heidegger: "Only because the Being of the 'there' receives its Constitution through understanding and through the character of understanding as projection, only because it *is* what it becomes (or alternatively, does not become), can it say to itself *'Become what you are'*, and say this with understanding." (Martin Heidegger, *Being and Time*, transl. John Macquarrie & Edward Robinson [NY: Harper & Row, 1962], Section 31, pp. 185-6).

15. "For me – how should there be any outside – myself? There is no outside." (Nietzsche, "The Convalescent," in the Third Part of *Thus Spoke Zarathustra*, appearing in *The Portable Nietzsche*, ed. and transl. Walter Kaufmann [NY: Penguin Books, 1968], p. 329).

16. See the last section (#1067, from the year 1885) of the collection of Nietzsche's unpublished fragments, *The Will to Power*, transl. Walter Kaufmann and R. J. Hollingdale, ed. Walter Kaufmann (NY: Vintage Books, 1968), p. 550.

17. Laurence Lampert: "Although Heidegger's lectures perform the great service of affording access to the encompassing scope of Nietzsche's thought, and although they pose the fundamental question that Zarathustra himself invites his audience to pose, there is no reason to be satisfied with Heidegger's answer, an answer that comes too soon, without consideration of the chapters in part III that exhibit the teaching of eternal return as the letting be of beings." (Lampert, *Nietzsche's Teaching: An Interpretation of Thus Spoke Zarathustra* [New Haven: Yale University Press, 1986], p. 150). Lampert also tells us later in his book: "Although Zarathustra's highest act is always presented as a commanding act of will, that mastering will blesses beings as they are. The highest commanding appears as an allowing ..." (Ibid., p. 221)

18. See, for example, the first section of the "Epilogue" of Nietzsche's *Nietzsche contra Wagner*: "*Amor fati*: that is my inmost nature." (*The Portable Nietzsche*, op. cit., p. 680). See also the last paragraph of "Why I Am So Clever" in *Ecce Homo*: "My formula for greatness in a human being is *Amor fati*." (Ibid., p. 258)

19. Concerning our acceptance of the repugnant, see especially the section "On Redemption" in the Second Part of Nietzsche's *Thus Spoke Zarathustra*.

20. The equation of eternity and time is most explicit in "The Drunken Song," just before the final chapter of *Zarathustra*.

21. "'I led you away from these fables when I taught you, "The will is a creator." All "it was" is a fragment, a riddle, a dreadful accident – until the creative will says to it, "But thus I willed it."'" ("On Redemption,"

The Portable Nietzsche, op. cit., p. 253). "To redeem those who lived in the past and to recreate all 'it was' into a 'thus I willed it' – that alone should I call redemption." (Ibid., p. 251) See also Section 3 of "On Old and New Tablets," ibid., p. 310.

22. See, for instance, the section "The Shadow" in the Fourth Part of *Thus Spoke Zarathustra*.

23. "Let me speak to them of what is most contemptible: but that is the *last man*." ("Zarathustra's Prologue," First Part of *Thus Spoke Zarathustra*, in *The Portable Nietzsche*, op. cit., p. 129). See also the chapter "The Ugliest Man" in the Fourth Part of *Zarathustra*.

24. "Instruments and toys are sense and spirit: behind them still lies the self. The self also seeks with the eyes of the senses; it also listens with the ears of the spirit. Always the self listens and seeks: it compares, overpowers, conquers, destroys. It controls, and it is in control of the ego too.

   "Behind your thoughts, my brother, there stands a mighty ruler, an unknown sage – whose name is self. In your body he dwells; he is your body.

   "There is more reason in your body than in your best wisdom. And who knows why your body needs precisely your best wisdom?

   "Your self laughs at your ego and at its bold leaps." (Nietzsche, "On the Despisers of the Body," *Zarathustra*, in *The Portable Nietzsche*, op. cit., pp. 146-7.)

25. See Chapter III, "The Elements of the 'Numinous': Creature-Feeling," in Otto's *The Idea of the Holy*, transl. John Harvey (London: Oxford University Press, 1958). For example: "There you have a self-confessed 'feeling of dependence', which is yet at the same time far more than, and something other than, *merely* a feeling of dependence. Desiring to give it a name of its own, I propose to call it 'creature-consciousness' or creature-feeling. It is the emotion of a creature, submerged and overwhelmed by its own nothingness in contrast to that which is supreme above all creatures." (pp. 9-10)

26. See Chapters IV and V of Otto's *The Idea of the Holy*, op. cit..

27. Otto: "'Love,' says one of the mystics, 'is nothing else than quenched wrath." (*The Idea of the Holy*, op. cit., p. 24)

28. For Otto's treatment of the Book of Job, see Chapter X ("The Numinous in the Old Testament") in *The Idea of the Holy*.

29. Nietzsche, *Ecce Homo*, transl. Walter Kaufmann, in *On the Genealogy of Morals and Ecce Homo*, op. cit., pp. 295-8.

30. Ibid., pp. 300-301.

31. Jung: "At last I had found confirmation that there were or had been people who saw evil and its universal power, and – more important – the mysterious role it played in delivering man from darkness and suffering. To that extent Goethe became, in my eyes, a prophet." (Jung, *Memories, Dreams, Reflections*, op. cit., p. 60). "I was carried away by enthusiasm, and soon afterward read *Thus Spoke Zarathustra*. This, like Goethe's

Faust, was a tremendous experience for me.   *Zarathustra* was Nietzsche's *Faust* ..." (Ibid., p. 102).

32.   Ibid., p. 294.

33.   Jung: "Nietzsche had been on my program for some time, but I hesitated to begin reading him because I felt I was insufficiently prepared. At that time he was much discussed, most in adverse terms, by the allegedly competent philosophy students ... I was held back by a secret fear that I might perhaps be like him, at least in regard to the 'secret' which had isolated him from his environment ... In spite of these trepidations I was curious, and finally resolved to read him. *Thoughts Out of Season* was the first volume that fell into my hands. I was carried away by enthusiasm, and soon afterward read *Thus Spake Zarathustra*. This, like Goethe's *Faust*, was a tremendous experience for me. *Zarathustra* was Nietzsche's *Faust*, his No. 2, and my No. 2 now corresponded to *Zarathustra* – though this was rather like comparing a molehill with Mount Blanc. And *Zarathustra* – there could be no doubt about that – was morbid. Was my No. 2 also morbid?" (Ibid., pp. 101-102.)

34.   See the chapter "Sigmund Freud" in Jung's *Memories, Dreams, Reflections*.

35.   See the chapter "Confrontation with the Unconscious," ibid., pp. 175-6.

36.   Jung: "I stood helpless before an alien world; everything in it seemed difficult and incomprehensible. I was living in a constant state of tension; often I felt as if gigantic blocks of stone were tumbling down upon me. One thunderstorm followed another. My enduring these storms was a question of brute strength.   Others have been shattered by them – Nietzsche, and Hölderlin, and many others." (Ibid., p. 177).

37.   William James, *The Varieties of Religious Experience: A Study in Human Nature* (NY: A Mentor Book, New American Library, 1958), pp. 376-377.

38.   See Don Cupitt, *The Sea of Faith: Christianity in Change* (London: British Broadcasting Corporation, 1985), p. 180: "Jung ... made one-man religions respectable by inventing his own and living it himself ... Jung represents religion at its most privatised." See also Cupitt's BBC video *The Sea of Faith*. Cupitt tells us in his accompanying text: "The Jungians draw attention to widespread cross-cultural patterns of symbolism, and suggest that they reflect certain deep predispositions in the human psyche." (*The Sea of Faith*, p. 257).

39.   Reiner Schürmann, *Meister Eckhart: Mystic and Philosopher – Translations and Commentary* (Bloomington and London: Indiana University Press, 1978), pp. 191-203.

40.   Ibid., pp. 13-19.

41.   Ibid., pp. 42-47, 159-168.

42.   For the notion of creative illness, see Henri Ellenberger, *The Discovery of the Unconscious: The History and Evolution of Dynamic Psychiatry* (NY: Basic Books, 1970), pp. 670-673.

43.   Jung: "Nietzsche had lost the ground under his feet because he possessed nothing more than the inner world of his thoughts – which incidentally possessed him more than he it. He was uprooted and hovered above the earth, and therefore he succumbed to exaggeration and irreality. For me, such irreality was the quintessence of horror, for I aimed, after all, at *this* world and *this* life. No matter how deeply absorbed or how blown about I was, I always knew that everything I experienced was ultimately directed at this real life of mine. I meant to meet its obligations and fulfill its meanings. My watchword was: *Hic Rhodus, hic salta!*" (*Memories, Dreams, Reflections*, op. cit., p. 189)

44.   The excerpt from Nietzsche's poem above is quoted and translated in Footnote 10 in Volume I of Jung's published Seminar: C. G. Jung, *Nietzsche's Zarathustra: Notes of the Seminar Given in 1934-1939 by C. G. Jung*, ed. James L. Jarrett, Bollingen Series XCIX (Princeton: Princeton University Press, 1988), p. 10.

45.   For an overall view of the life and thought of Paul Tillich, see Wilhelm and Marion Pauck, *Paul Tillich: His Life and Thought* (NY: Harper & Row, 1976), as well as *The Thought of Paul Tillich*, eds. James Luther Adams, Wilhelm Pauck, and Roger Lincoln Shinn (NY: Harper & Row, 1985).

46.   See Paul Tillich, *Systematic Theology, Volume I* (Chicago: University of Chicago Press, 1951), pp. 81-2.

47.   See Michael F. Palmer, *Paul Tillich's Philosophy of Art* (NY-Berlin: Walter de Gruyter, 1984), p. 137, pp. 65-6.

48.   See Paul Tillich, *Systematic Theology, Volume I*, op. cit., pp. 65-6.

49.   See Paul Tillich, *Systematic Theology, Volume III: Life and the Spirit, History, and the Kingdom of God* (Chicago: University of Chicago Press, 1951), pp. 157-161.

50.   See Paul Tillich, *The Courage to Be* (New Haven: Yale University Press, 1952), esp. pp. 40-54.

51.   Ibid., p. 4, p. 6.

52.   Ibid., pp. 156-7.

53.   Ibid., pp. 179-181.

54.   Ibid., p. 190.

55.   See Paul Tillich, *Systematic Theology, Vol. II*, op. cit., pp. 118-135, 165-168.

56.   See Paul Tillich, *The Meaning of Health: Essays in Existentialism, Psychoanalysis and Religion*, ed. Perry Le Fevre (Chicago: Chicago Theological Seminary Exploration Press, 1984), p. 182.

57.   Ibid., p. 150.

58.   Ibid., p. 171.

59.   Quoted in *Dürckheim – Dialogue on the Path of Initiation: An Introduction to the Life and Thought of Karlfried Graf Dürckheim*, by Alphonse Goettmann (NY: Globe Press Books, 1991), p. 10.

60.   Ibid..

61. Ibid., p. 10.

62. Ibid., pp. 11-13.

63. Ibid., pp. 22-3.

64. Ibid., p. 23.

65. For Dürckheim's comments on the "experience of transcendence", see *Dürckheim – Dialogue on the Path of Initiation*, op. cit., p. 53. For the need for "discernment" in the "experience of transcendence," see the same text, pp. 72-73. As Dürckheim tells his interlocutor Goettmann in this book: "The latter ['the consciousness of the body that we have'] is directed toward health and perhaps beauty, whereas the former ['experience of transcendence'] is oriented toward transparence to our transcendent core." (p. 86). See also p. 150.

66. Paul's statement in *Galatians* 2:20 is quoted in *Dürckheim – Dialogue on the Path of Initiation*, op. cit., p. 40.

67. Ibid., p. 43ff.

68. Dürckheim: "My anthropology sees man as a being conscious of himself, suffering first of all from not being what he is in reality. This is the man who has overdeveloped his existential self and one day must learn to transcend it in order to rediscover his deeper self. We could say that man evolves through three kinds of 'self':

"— the 'little self' who only sees power, security, prestige, knowledge.

"— the 'existential self' who goes much further; it wants to give itself to a cause, to a work, to a community, to a person. It can go beyond egocentrism, and that is where it becomes, in my opinion, a human being.

"— finally, what I call the 'essential self', the true 'I' of the individual and of humanity." (Ibid., p. 40)

69. Ibid., pp. 44-5.

70. Ibid., pp. 94-6.

71. Ibid., p. 96.

72. Ibid., p. 80.

73. Ibid., pp. 74-8.

74. See Paul Tillich, *The Shaking of the Foundations* (NY: Charles Scribner & Sons, 1948), pp. 149-163.

75. Ibid., p. 140.

76. See Alphonse Goettmann's Introduction in *Dürckheim – Dialogue on the Path of Initiation*, op. cit., p. xiii.

77. Dürckheim: "But let us not forget that an experience of awakening does not create an awakened person." (Ibid., p. 126)

78. Ibid., p. 121.

79. Ibid., pp. 119-120.

80. Nietzsche, *Beyond Good and Evil: Prelude to a Philosophy of the Future*, transl. Walter Kaufmann (NY: Vintage Books, A Division of Random House), Part IV: "Epigrams and Interludes," Aphorism 146, p. 89.

81. See the *Zusatz* (additional commentary) to Paragraph 212 of Hegel's *Encyclopedia Logic*, at the end of his section on "Teleology." (*Hegel's*

Logic: Being Part One of The Encyclopedia of the Philosophical Sciences (1830), transl. William Wallace with an Introduction by J. N. Findlay [Oxford: Clarendon Press, 1989], p. 274).

82. Related to this treatment of philosophy, and especially in philosophies of antiquity, is Martha Nussbaum's book *The Therapy of Desire: Theory and Practice in Hellenistic Ethics* (Princeton: Princeton University Press, 1994). As Nussbaum states toward the beginning of her Introduction: "The Hellenistic philosophical schools in Greece and Rome – Epicureans, Skeptics, and Stoics – all conceived of philosophy as a way of addressing the most painful problems of human life. They saw the philosopher as a compassionate physician whose arts could heal many pervasive types of human suffering. They practiced philosophy not as a detached intellectual technique dedicated to the display of cleverness but as an immersed and worldly art of grappling with human misery." (p. 3)

83. Pierre Hadot, "Forms of Life and Forms of Discourse," *Philosophy as a Way of Life: Spiritual Exercises from Socrates to Foucault*, transl. Michael Chase (Oxford: Basil Blackwell Ltd., 1995), p. 69.

84. Pierre Hadot, "Spiritual Exercises," ibid., p. 85.

Part Two: Exploring the Mystery of Timelessness

1. For background of Taoism in Chinese history, see Huston Smith, *The World's Religions* (NY: HarperCollins, 1991), pp. 196-220, along with John B. Noss and David S. Noss, *Man's Religions*, 7th ed. (NY: Macmillan, 1986), pp. 234-264.

2. Jung's Terry Lectures are included, under the title of "Psychology and Religion," at the beginning of Part One of Volume 11 (*Psychology and Religion: East and West*) of *The Collected Works of C. G. Jung*, eds. Sir Herbert Read, Michael Fordham, Gerhard Adler, and William McGuire, Bollingen Series (Princeton: Princeton University Press, 1969), pp. 5-105. Jung's Terry Lectures were originally published in English as *The Terry Lectures of 1937* (New Haven: Yale University Press and London: Oxford University Press, 1938).

3. On Zaehner and Jung, see Barry Ulanov, *Jung and the Outside World* (Wilmette, IL: Chiron Publications, 1992), pp. 228-243.

4. *Tao Te Ching: A New English Version*, transl. Stephen Mitchell (New York: HarperCollins Publishers, Harper & Row Publishers, 1988), Poem 56. Hereafter cited by the translator's name.

5. Ludwig Wittgenstein, *Tractatus Logico-Philosophicus*, transl. C. K. Ogden with an Introduction by Bertrand Russell (London and NY: Routledge, 1990), pp. 188-189 (Proposition 7).

6. Ibid., p. 187 (Proposition 6.522).

7. Quoted in John Caputo, *The Mystical Element in Heidegger's Thought* (Athens: Ohio University Press, 1978), p. 192.

8. Mitchell, op. cit., Poem 41.

9. Ibid., Poem 37.
10. Ibid., Poem 42.
11. Ibid.
12. See Fritjof Capra, *The Tao of Physics* (NY: Bantam Books, 1988), esp. pp. 96-97.
13. See Herbert R. Coursen, *The Compensatory Psyche: A Jungian Approach to Shakespeare* (Lanham,MD: University Press of America, 1986).
14. Frank Lloyd Wright: "Now, where did the thought in all this new Architecture come from? Well, we must admit that it has been lying long in the great philosophies of all the ages. But Lao-tzu, the Chinese philosopher, first called attention to the actual thing when he declared (some five hundred years before Jesus, I think it was), 'The reality of the building does not consist in the four walls and the roof but in the space within to be lived in.' And right there is the central core of this work of the Mind which we call 'Organic Architecture.' That simple assertion by Lao-tzu is the philosophic center line of our Organic Architecture. Were you to expand that central thought *naturally*, were you to take it to heart as it *is* in itself, it would turn everything you have been taught and everything you see around you upside down and inside out. It is quite impossible for me, here in the time at our disposal to give you more than a mere hint of the tremendous change, the great importance to our future that comes into the life of any individual who begins to *think* thus – *from the within outward*." (From Wright's lecture "The Architect," 1946, in *Frank Lloyd Wright: Collected Writings, Volume 4, 1939-1949*, ed. Bruce Brooks Pfeiffer [NY: Rizzoli International Publications, Inc., 1994], p. 288.)
15. Martin Heidegger: "When we fill the jug, the pouring that fills it flows into the empty jug. The emptiness, the void, is what does the vessel's holding. The empty space, this nothing of the jug, is what the jug is as the holding vessel ... The jug's void determines all the handling in the process of making the vessel. The vessel's thingness does not lie at all in the material of which it consists, but in the void that holds." ("The Thing," in the collection *Poetry, Language, Thought*, transl. Albert Hofstadter [NY: Harper & Row,1971], p. 169).
16. Mitchell, op. cit., Poem 28.
17. Ibid., Poem 15.
18. Ibid., Poem 22.
19. Ibid., Poem 12.
20. Ibid., Poem 54.
21. Jung: "And *Sinn* can also be translated by 'meaning'; Wilhelm translates *Tao* 'meaning.'" (*Nietzsche's Zarathustra*, op. cit., p. 385).
22. John Keats, *Letter to George and Thomas Keats, 28 Dec. 1817*, in *The Quotation Dictionary*, ed. Robin Hyman (NY: The Macmillan Company, 1962), p. 151.

23.   Martin Heidegger: "What seems easier than to let a being be just the being that it is? Or does this turn out to be the most difficult of tasks, particularly if such an intention – to let a being be as it is – represents the opposite of the indifferent that simply turns its back upon the being itself in favor of an unexamined concept of being? We ought to turn toward the being, think about it in regard to its being, but by means of this thinking at the same time let it rest upon itself in its very own being." (Martin Heidegger, "The Origin of the Work of Art," from the collection *Poetry, Language, Thought*, op. cit., p. 31.)

24.   For an excellent discussion of "meditation complex" see Jungian analyst and Zen meditator V. Walter Odajnyk, *Gathering the Light: A Psychology of Meditation* (Boston and London: Shambala, 1993), pp. 85-90.

25.   Barbarah Hannah, *Jung: His Life and Work (A Biographical Memoir)* (NY: Capricorn Books, G. P. Putnam's Sons, 1976), p. 128.

26.   Jung: "In the end the only events in my life worth telling are those when the imperishable world irrupted into this transitory one."   (Jung, *Memories, Dreams, Reflections*, op. cit., Prologue, p. 4)

27.   See Jung's "Foreword" to Erich Neumann, *The Origins and History of Consciousness*, Part I: "The Psychological Stages and the Evolution of Consciousness" of Volume I   (NY: Harper Torchbooks/The Bollingen Library, 1962), pp. xiii-xiv.

28.   Jung, *Memories, Dreams, Reflections*, op. cit., p. 206.

29.   Ibid., p. 20.

30.   Ibid..

31.   Ibid., pp. 196-7.

32.   Ibid., pp. 197-199.

33.   Ibid., p. 208.

34.   Mitchell, op. cit., Poem 20.

35.   Jung, *Memories, Dreams, Reflections*, op. cit., p. 359.

36.   Saint Augustine, *Confessions*, transl. Henry Chadwick (NY: Oxford University Press, 1991), p. 43.

37.   Jung: "For Buddha, the self stands above all gods, a *unus mundus* which represents the essence of human existence and of the world as a whole. The Self embodies both the aspect of intrinsic being and the aspect of its being known, without which no world exists." (*Memories, Dreams, Reflections*, op. cit., p. 279).

38.   Ibid., pp. 395-6.

39.   See *Saint Thomas Aquinas: Philosophical Texts*, selected and translated by Thomas Gilby (NY: Oxford University Press, 1960), p. 30 (#80) and p. 320 (#928).

EPILOGUE:
THE FUTURE OF JUNG'S PSYCHOLOGY

1. This informal talk took place on October 16, 2001, at Bowdoin College in Brunswick, Maine.

2. James H. Austin, *Zen And The Brain: Toward an Understanding of Meditation and Consciousness* (Cambridge, MA: MIT Press, 1998).

3. *Atom And Archetype: The Pauli-Jung Letters 1932-1958*, ed. C.A. Meier, Preface by Beverley Zabriskie (Princeton, NJ: Princeton University Press, 2001).

4. For an especially relevant exposition of this view, see Anthony Stevens, *The Roots Of War: A Jungian Perspective* (New York: Paragon House, 1989), pp. 56-57, 217-218.

5. See Samuel P. Huntington, *The Clash Of Civilizations And The Remaking Of World Order* (New York: Simon & Schuster-Touchstone, 1997), pp. 19-78, 301-321.

6. See Karen Armstrong, *Islam: A Short History* (NY: The Modern Library, 2000), p. 201.

7. Jung. "Psychotherapists or the Clergy," in Volume 11 of *The Collected Works of C. G. Jung*, op. cit., par. 509, p. 334.

8. Eugene Taylor, Shadow Culture: Psychology and Spirituality in America (Washington, DC: Counterpoint, 1999).

9. Austin, op. cit., p. 15.

10. Huston Smith, *The World's Religions*, 2nd Edition (New York: Harper-Collins, 1991), pp. 1-11. See also Huston Smith, *Forgotten Truth: The Primordial Tradition* (New York: Harper and Row, 1976). Compare Aldous Huxley, *The Perennial Philosophy* (New York and London: Harper and Brothers, 1945), pp. vii-xi, 1-35.

11. See Otto's *The Idea Of The Holy*, op.cit., 175-229, and also his comparative study of the monistic and unitary mysticisms of Meister Eckhart and Shankara in *Mysticism East And West* (Meridian Books, 1957).

12. See Jung, *Memories, Dreams, Reflections*, op. cit., "Glossary" (p. 395, p. 398) and Ch. XII, "Late Thoughts," and "Retrospect." See also Edward F. Edinger, M.D., *Ego and Archetype* (Baltimore, MD: Pelican Books, 1973), pp. 1-96.

13. For additional philosophical context, see Alexander Nehemas, *The Art Of Living: Socratic Reflections from Plato to Foucault*, esp. Ch. 6, "A Fate for Socrates' Reason: Foucault on the Care of the Self" (Berkeley: University of California Press, 1998), pp. 158-188, and Alexander Nehemas, *Virtues Of Authenticity: Essays on Plato and Socrates* (Princeton, N.J.: Princeton University Press, 1999), esp. Part I: "Socrates: Questions of Goodness and Method," pp. 3-107.

14. C.G. Jung, "On 'The Tibetan Book of the Great Liberation'," in Volume 11 of *The Collected Works of C. G. Jung*, op. cit., par. 773, p. 484.

15. Austin, op. cit., p. 611.

16. Jung, "Psychology And Religion" (Terry Lectures), in Volume 11 of *The Collected Works of C. G. Jung*, op.cit., part. 69, p. 41.

17. Ibid., p. 584.

18. Austin, op. cit., p. 66.

19. See Austin, op. cit., pp. 574-75, and Jung, *Memories, Dreams, Reflections*, op. cit., Ch. 10, "Visions", pp. 289-298.

20. Jung, *Memories*, op. cit., p. 295, p. 296.

21. Ibid., p. 297. Austin cites the art of Edward Hopper and Giorgio di Chirico to illustrate the impersonal objectivity of the "lunar" view (Austin, op. cit., p. 577).

22. Austin, op. cit., pp. 43-47. For a "pragmatic" view of Zen similar to Austin's, see *Bridging the I-System: Unifying Spirituality and Behavior* by two experienced Zen practitioners, Stanley H. Block, M.D. and Carolyn Bryant Block (White Cloud Press: Ashland, Oregon, 2002).

23. Austin, op. cit., p. 610, figure 19.

24. Ibid., pp. 660-663.

25. See Austin, op. cit., pp. 660-663, and also Edinger, *Ego and Archetype*, pp. 2-104.

26. Jung, Volume 6, *The Collected Works of C. G. Jung* (Princeton/ Bollingen Series), par. 708.

27. Austin, op. cit., pp. 660-663.

28. Ibid., p. 528.

29. *Atom And Archetype*, op. cit., p. 5, p. 10.

30. Ibid., Preface, p. xxvii.

31. Ibid., pp. xxxviii-xxxix.

32. Ibid., p. 83, p. 87.

33. Ibid., p. 110, p. 112.

34. See Beverley Zabriskie, *Atom and Archetype*, op.cit., "Introductory Essay: Quantum Science and Alchemy," pp. xxxv-xxxvi. Compare the central Buddhist concept of *Pratitya-samutpāda*, a Sanskrit term for "interdependent arising" or "origination." See also *The Shambala Dictionary Of Buddhism And Zen*, transl. Michael H. Kohn (Boston: Shambala, 1991), p. 172.

35. *Atom and Archetype*, op. cit., pp. 73-74.

36. *The New York Times*, March 12, 2002, A5.

37. Cf. Austin, op. cit., p 15.

38. Merriam Websters's Collegiate Dictionary, 10ᵗʰ Edition, p. 785.

39. A striking contemporary example of intuition into the creative potential of the collective or universal unconscious and its *complexio oppositorum* can be seen in the case of the mathematical genius, Nobel Laureate, and recovered schizophrenic John Forbes Nash, Jr.. Nash has recently emerged into America's popular consciousness with Sylvia Nasar's

biography *A Beautiful Mind*, but most especially with Ron Howard's Oscar-winning film adaptation of that biography. In 1959 Nash was conversing with another mathematician, Harvard Professor George Mackey, who asked him: "'How could you ... a mathematician, a man devoted to reason and logical proof ... how could you believe that extraterrestrials are sending you messages? How could you believe that you are being recruited by aliens from outer space to save the world?'" Nash looked up at last and fixed Mackey with an unblinking stare as cool and dispassionate as that of any bird or snake. "Because," Nash said slowly in soft, reasonable southern drawl, as if talking to himself, "the ideas I had about supernatural beings came to me the same way that my mathematical ideas did. So I took them seriously.'" See Sylvia Nasar, *A Beautiful Mind: The Life of Mathematical Genius and Nobel Laureate John Nash* (New York, NY: Touchstone, 1998), Prologue, p. 1.

40. *Atom and Archetype*, op. cit., pp. 75-76, pp. 85-86.

41. Cited in Austin, op.cit., p. 548.

42. See Deirdre Carabine, *The Unknown God: Negative Theology in the Platonic Tradition: Plato to Eriugena,* Louvain Theological and Pastoral Monographs 19 (Peeters Press Louvain W.B. Eerdmans, n.d).

43. H.J. Chadwick, *The Imitation Of Christ* (Bridge-Logos, 1999), p. 148.

44. Jung, *Nietzsche's Zarathustra*, op. cit., Vol. II, p. 1365.

45. Elie Humbert, *C. G. Jung: The Fundamentals of Theory and Practice*, transl. Ronald G. Jalbert (Wilmette, IL: Chiron Publications, 1988), pp. 9-13.

WORKS CITED

Adams, James Luther, Wilhelm Pauck, and Roger Lincoln Shinn, eds., *The Thought of Paul Tillich* (NY: Harper & Row, 1985).

Aquinas, Thomas, *Saint Thomas Aquinas: Philosophical Texts*, selected and translated by Thomas Gilby (NY: Oxford University Press, 1960).

Armstrong, Karen, *Islam: A Short History* (NY: The Modern Library, 2000).

Augustine, *Confessions*, transl. Henry Chadwick (NY: Oxford University Press, 1991).

Austin, James H., *Zen And The Brain: Toward an Understanding of Meditation and Consciousness* (Cambridge, MA: MIT Press, 1998).

Baynes, H. G., *Analytical Psychology and the English Mind* (London: Methuen and Co., Ltd., 1950).

Block, Stanley H. and Carolyn Bryant, *Bridging the I-System: Unifying Spirituality and Behavior* (White Cloud Press: Ashland, Oregon, 2002).

Capra, Fritjof, *The Tao of Physics* (NY: Bantam Books, 1988).

Caputo, John, *The Mystical Element in Heidegger's Thought* (Athens: Ohio University Press, 1978).

Carabine, Deirdre, *The Unknown God: Negative Theology in the Platonic Tradition: Plato to Eriugena,* Louvain Theological and Pastoral Monographs 19 (Peeters Press Louvain W.B. Eerdmans, n.d).

Chadwick, H. J., *The Imitation Of Christ* (Bridge-Logos, 1999).

Church, F. Forrester, ed., *The Essential Tillich: An Anthology of the Writings of Paul Tillich* (NY: Macmillan Publishing Company, 1987).

Coursen, Herbert R., *The Compensatory Psyche: A Jungian Approach to Shakespeare* (Lanham,MD: University Press of America, 1986).

Cupitt, Don, *The Sea of Faith: Christianity in Change* (London: British Broadcasting Corporation, 1985).

Edinger, Edward F., *Ego and Archetype* (Baltimore, MD: Pelican Books, 1973).

Ellenberger, Henri, *The Discovery of the Unconscious: The History and Evolution of Dynamic Psychiatry* (NY: Basic Books, 1970).

Geoghegan, William D., *Platonism in Recent Religious Thought* (New York: Columbia University Press, 1958).

Goettmann, Alphonse, ed., *Dürckheim – Dialogue on the Path of Initiation: An Introduction to the Life and Thought of Karlfried Graf Dürckheim* (NY: Globe Press Books, 1991).

Hadot, Pierre, *Philosophy as a Way of Life: Spiritual Exercises from Socrates to Foucault*, transl. Michael Chase (Oxford: Basil Blackwell Ltd., 1995).

Hannah, Barbara, *Jung: His Life and Work (A Biographical Memoir)* (NY: Capricorn Books, G. P. Putnam's Sons, 1976).

Hegel, G. W. F., *Hegel's Logic: Being Part One of The Encyclopedia of the Philosophical Sciences (1830)*, transl. William Wallace with an Introduction by J. N. Findlay (Oxford: Clarendon Press, 1989).

Hegel, G. W. F., *The Phenomenology of Mind*, transl. J. B. Baillie (NY: Harper Torchbooks, Harper and Row, 1967).

Heidegger, Martin, *Being and Time*, transl. John Macquarrie & Edward Robinson (NY: Harper & Row, 1962).

Heidegger, Martin, *Poetry, Language, Thought*, transl. Albert Hofstadter (NY: Harper & Row, 1971).

Holy Bible, The: Revised Standard Edition.

Humbert, Elie, *C. G. Jung: The Fundamentals of Theory and Practice*, transl. Ronald G. Jalbert (Wilmette, IL: Chiron Publications, 1988).

Huntington, Samuel P., *The Clash Of Civilizations And The Remaking Of World Order* (New York: Simon & Schuster-Touchstone, 1997).

Huxley, Aldous, *The Perennial Philosophy* (New York and London: Harper and Brothers, 1945).

James, William, *The Varieties of Religious Experience: A Study in Human Nature* (NY: A Mentor Book, New American Library, 1958).

Jung, Carl Gustav, *Memories, Dreams, Reflections*, ed. Aniela Jaffé, transl. Richard and Clara Winston, Revised Edition (NY: Vintage Books, A Division of Random House, 1965).

Jung, Carl Gustav, *Nietzsche's Zarathustra: Notes of the Seminar Given in 1934-1939 by C. G. Jung*, ed. James L. Jarrett, Bollingen Series XCIX (Princeton: Princeton University Press, 1988).

Jung, Carl Gustav, *Psychology and Religion: West and East*, 2nd Edition, Vol. 11 Bollingen Series 20 (Princeton, NJ: Princeton University Press, 1969).

Jung, Carl Gustav, *The Collected Works of C. G. Jung*, Bollingen Series XX (Princeton: Princeton University Press, 1969).

Keats, John, *Letter to George and Thomas Keats, 28 Dec. 1817*, in *The Quotation Dictionary*, ed. Robin Hyman (NY: The Macmillan Company, 1962).

Kohn, Michael H., ed. and transl., *The Shambala Dictionary Of Buddhism And Zen*, (Boston: Shambala, 1991).

Lampert, Laurence, *Nietzsche's Teaching: An Interpretation of Thus Spoke Zarathustra* (New Haven: Yale University Press, 1986) .

Lao-tze, *Tao Te Ching: A New English Version*, transl. Stephen Mitchell (New York: HarperCollins Publishers, Harper & Row Publishers, 1988).

Meier, C. A., ed., Atom *And Archetype: The Pauli-Jung Letters 1932-1958*, Preface by Beverley Zabriskie (Princeton, NJ: Princeton University Press, 2001).

Merleau-Ponty, Maurice, *Sense and Non-sense* (Northwestern University Press, 1964).

Nasar, Sylvia, *A Beautiful Mind: The Life of Mathematical Genius and Nobel Laureate John Nash* (New York, NY: Touchstone, 1998).

Nehemas, Alexander, *The Art Of Living: Socratic Reflections from Plato to Foucault* (Berkeley: University of California Press, 1998).

Nehemas, Alexander, *Virtues Of Authenticity: Essays on Plato and Socrates* (Princeton, N.J.: Princeton University Press, 1999).

Neumann, Erich, *The Origins and History of Consciousness* (NY: Harper Torchbooks/The Bollingen Library, 1962).

Nietzsche, Friedrich, *Beyond Good and Evil: Prelude to a Philosophy of the Future*, transl. Walter Kaufmann (NY: Vintage Books, A Division of Random House).

Nietzsche, Friedrich, *Ecce Homo*, transl. and ed. Walter Kaufmann, appearing in *On the Genealogy of Morals and Ecce Homo* (NY: Vintage Books, Random House).

Nietzsche, Friedrich, *Nietzsche contra Wagner*, appearing in *The Portable Nietzsche*, ed. and transl. Walter Kaufmann (NY: Penguin Books, 1968).

Nietzsche, Friedrich, *The Will to Power*, transl. Walter Kaufmann and R. J. Hollingdale, ed. Walter Kaufmann (NY: Vintage Books, 1968).

Nietzsche, Friedrich, *Thus Spoke Zarathustra*, appearing in *The Portable Nietzsche*, ed. and transl. Walter Kaufmann (NY: Penguin Books, 1968).

Noss, John B. and David S., *Man's Religions*, 7th ed. (NY: Macmillan, 1986).

Nussbaum, Martha, *The Therapy of Desire: Theory and Practice in Hellenistic Ethics* (Princeton: Princeton University Press, 1994).

Odajnyk, V. Walter, *Gathering the Light: A Psychology of Meditation* (Boston and London: Shambala, 1993).

Otto, Rudolf, *Mysticism East And West* (Meridian Books, 1957).

Otto, Rudolf, *The Idea of the Holy*, transl. John Harvey (London: Oxford University Press, 1958).

Palmer, Michael F., *Paul Tillich's Philosophy of Art* (NY-Berlin: Walter de Gruyter, 1984).

Pauck, Wilhelm and Marion, *Paul Tillich: His Life and Thought* (NY: Harper & Row, 1976).

Rilke, Rainer Maria, *Letters to a Young Poet* (1903), transl. Stephen Mitchell (NY: Random House, 1984).

Schürmann, Reiner, *Meister Eckhart: Mystic and Philosopher – Translations and Commentary* (Bloomington and London: Indiana University Press, 1978).

Smith, Huston, *Forgotten Truth: The Primordial Tradition* (New York: Harper and Row, 1976).

Smith, Huston, *The World's Religions*, 2nd Edition (New York: Harper-Collins, 1991).

Stevens, Anthony, *The Roots Of War: A Jungian Perspective* (New York: Paragon House, 1989).

Taylor, Charles, *Hegel* (Cambridge: Cambridge University Press, 1991).

Taylor, Eugene, *Shadow Culture: Psychology and Spirituality in America* (Washington, DC: Counterpoint, 1999).

Tillich, Paul, *Systematic Theology, Volume I* (Chicago: University of Chicago Press, 1951).

Tillich, Paul, *Systematic Theology, Vol. II: Existence and the Christ* (Chicago: University of Chicago Press, 1957).

Tillich, Paul, *Systematic Theology, Volume III: Life and the Spirit, History, and the Kingdom of God* (Chicago: University of Chicago Press, 1951).

Tillich, Paul, *The Courage to Be* (New Haven: Yale University Press, 1952).

Tillich, Paul, *The Courage To Be*, Second Edition, with an Introduction by Peter J. Gomes (New Haven and London: Yale University Press, 2000).

Tillich, Paul, *The Meaning of Health: Essays in Existentialism, Psychoanalysis and Religion*, ed. Perry Le Fevre (Chicago: Chicago Theological Seminary Exploration Press, 1984).

Tillich, Paul, *The Protestant Era* (Chicago: University of Chicago Press, 1957).

Tillich, Paul, *The Shaking of the Foundations* (NY: Charles Scribner & Sons, 1948).

Ulanov, Barry, *Jung and the Outside World* (Wilmette, IL: Chiron Publications, 1992).

Wittgenstein, Ludwig, *Tractatus Logico-Philosophicus*, transl. C. K. Ogden with an Introduction by Bertrand Russell (London and NY: Routledge, 1990).

Wright, Frank Lloyd, *Frank Lloyd Wright: Collected Writings, Volume 4, 1939-1949*, ed. Bruce Brooks Pfeiffer (NY: Rizzoli International Publications, Inc., 1994).

Yeats, William Butler, *Selected Poems and Two Plays of William Butler Yeats*, ed. M. L. Rosenthal (NY: Collier Books, The Macmillan Company, 1962).

ABOUT THE CONTRIBUTORS

William D. Geoghegan was born on July 16, 1922, in Wilmington, Delaware. He received his Ph.D. in Philosophy of Religion from Columbia University in 1951, and he received his M. Div. degree (*magna cum laude*) from Drew Theological Seminary in 1945. He earned his B. A. at Yale University (1943), graduating *magna cum laude*.

Bill Geoghegan is Emeritus Professor of Religion at Bowdoin College in Brunswick, Maine, where he taught for four decades. His areas of research include Idealist Religious Thought, Analytical Psychology and Religion, Comparative Mysticism, and studies of the creative process in art, psychology, and religion. He published *Platonism in Recent Religious Thought* in 1958 (Columbia University Press) and has published numerous articles and reviews over the years. He is the founder of the Bowdoin College Jung Seminar (1980) and a co-founder of the Bowdoin-Brunswick C. G. Jung Center for Studies in Analytical Psychology (1988). He lives in Brunswick with his lovely wife Betty, to whom he has been married since 1946.

Kevin L. Stoehr was born on November 19, 1967, in Portland, Maine. He received his Ph.D. and M. A. degrees from the Department of Philosophy at Boston University in 1997. He earned his A.B. in philosophy at Bowdoin College, graduating *magna cum laude* in 1990.

Kevin has served since 1998 as Assistant Professor of Humanities and Rhetoric in the College of General Studies at Boston University. Previously, he taught humanities in the Core Curriculum at Boston University and served as Program Administrator and Coordinator of the 20th World Congress of Philosophy. He is the editor of two collections of essays – *Film and Knowledge: Essays on the Integration of Images and Ideas* (McFarland & Co. Publishers, 2002) and *Philosophies of Religion, Art, and Creativity: Volume IV of the Proceedings of the 20th World Congress of Philosophy* (Philosophy Documentation Center, 1999). He lives in Portland with his partner Sean.

COMMENTARY ON THIS BOOK

"The dialogue method flows and the book reads beautifully. It addresses a timely and important topic and certainly contains great wisdom and depth."
Murray Stein, Ph.D./ President, Intl. Assoc. of Analytical Psychology

"This spirited 'conversation' about ultimate concern in the tradition of Platonic dialogue is one of the most refreshing, challenging and instructive books that I have read in the last ten years or so. It is rooted in the wisdom of an esteemed professor who has sought, in the spirit of the German poet Rilke, to 'live the questions'. I highly recommend it as essential reading for any serious student of Jung's psychology."
Paul D. Huss, D. Min./ Pastoral Counselor, Jungian Analyst

"Engaged by this warm, highly inquisitive dialogue between a professor emeritus and his former student, an academic himself, our courage takes heart, and we join the two teachers to explore the spiritual crisis of our times ... As the dialogue progresses, our thinking is supported by the rhetorical frame, and we feel comforted by the generosity of the affection between professor and student. In the process, our philosophical resolve intensifies, and we grow keen to search the edges of being/non-being for our own way or ways. It is this inspirited keenness that is the gift of this book."
Walter R. Christie, M.D./, FAPA, Maine Medical Center

"After defining the spiritual problem of our age as nihilism, this book deftly cuts through to the harmonious threads of thinkers from the fourth century to the present. From Nietzsche, Jung, Tillich, Dürckheim and many others, the answer lies in finding spiritedness and the numinous in an experiential tapestry of self-realization, individuation and 'becoming what you are'. Carl Jung's psychology ties it all together and enhances spiritual growth."
Dean F. Davies, M.D., Ph.D./ Prof. of Community Medicine, Ret.

"It's an exceptional piece of work. William Geoghegan's mind shines forth in all of its brilliance. His power of integration is awesome. He truly 'lives the questions'. I've read the entire manuscript: it will never leave my side."
Rabbi Harry Sky